COMBINATION PRODUCTS

PART 4
REGULATION OF COMBINATION PRODUCTS

PART 210
CURRENT GOOD MANUFACTURING PRACTICE IN MANUFACTURING, PROCESSING, PACKING, OR HOLDING OF DRUGS; GENERAL

PART 211
CURRENT GOOD MANUFACTURING PRACTICE FOR FINISHED PHARMACEUTICALS

PART 820
QUALITY SYSTEM REGULATION

September 1, 2024

Founded in 2005, Business Excellence Consulting Inc. (BEC) offers consulting, remediation, auditing, regulatory affairs, and training services for the FDA-regulated industry. As a worldwide leading company, BEC covers all your compliance and regulatory needs for the pharmaceutical, biotech, medical device, combination product, API, cosmetic, and food industries.

BEC-GLOBAL
www.bec-global.com
info@bec-global.com
www.calidadpr.com
info@calidadpr.com

Ph: +1.787.705.7272

Main Office
Metro Medical Center, Torre B Suite 905
Bayamón, Puerto Rico, 0059 (USA)

Postal Address
P.O Box 8326,
Bayamón, PR, 00960-8326, (USA)

TITLE 21
FOOD AND DRUGS

CHAPTER I
FOOD AND DRUG ADMINISTRATION, DEPARTMENT OF HEALTH AND HUMAN SERVICES

SUBCHAPTER A - GENERAL

PART 4
REGULATION OF COMBINATION PRODUCTS

Subpart A - Current Good Manufacturing Practice Requirements for Combination Products

§ 4.1   What is the scope of this subpart?
§ 4.2   How does FDA define key terms and phrases in this subpart?
§ 4.3   What current good manufacturing practice requirements apply to my combination product?
§ 4.4   How can I comply with these current good manufacturing practice requirements for a co-packaged or single-entity combination product?

Subpart B - Postmarketing Safety Reporting for Combination Products

§ 4.100   What is the scope of this subpart?
§ 4.101   How does the FDA define key terms and phrases in this subpart?
§ 4.102   What reports must you submit to FDA for your combination product or constituent part?
§ 4.103   What information must you share with other constituent part applicants for the combination product?

§ 4.104 How and where must you submit postmarketing safety reports for your combination product or constituent part?

§ 4.105 What are the postmarketing safety reporting recordkeeping requirements for your combination product or constituent part?

Authority: 21 U.S.C. 321, 331, 351, 352, 353, 355, 360, 360b-360f, 360h-360j, 360l, 360hh-360ss, 360aaa-360bbb, 371(a), 372-374, 379e, 381, 383, 394; 42 U.S.C. 216, 262, 263a, 264, 271.

Source: 78 FR 4321, Jan. 22, 2013, unless otherwise noted.

SUBPART A - CURRENT GOOD MANUFACTURING PRACTICE REQUIREMENTS FOR COMBINATION PRODUCTS

§ 4.1 What is the scope of this subpart?

This subpart applies to combination products. It establishes which current good manufacturing practice requirements apply to these products. This subpart clarifies the application of current good manufacturing practice regulations to combination products, and provides a regulatory framework for designing and implementing the current good manufacturing practice operating system at facilities that manufacture co-packaged or single-entity combination products.

§ 4.2 How does FDA define key terms and phrases in this subpart?

The terms listed in this section have the following meanings for purposes of this subpart:

Biological product has the meaning set forth in § 3.2(d) of this chapter. A biological product also meets the definitions of either a drug or device as these terms are defined under this section.

Combination product has the meaning set forth in § 3.2(e) of this chapter.

Constituent part is a drug, device, or biological product that is part of a combination product.

Co-packaged combination product has the meaning set forth in § 3.2(e)(2) of this chapter.

Current good manufacturing practice operating system means the operating system within an establishment that is designed and implemented to address and meet the current good manufacturing practice requirements for a combination product.

Current good manufacturing practice requirements means the requirements set forth under § 4.3(a) through (d).

Device has the meaning set forth in § 3.2(f) of this chapter. A device that is a constituent part of a combination product is considered a finished device within the meaning of the QS regulation.

Drug has the meaning set forth in § 3.2(g) of this chapter. A drug that is a constituent part of a combination product is considered a drug product within the meaning of the drug CGMPs.

Drug CGMPs refers to the current good manufacturing practice regulations set forth in parts 210 and 211 of this chapter.

HCT/Ps refers to human cell, tissue, and cellular and tissue-based products, as defined in § 1271.3(d) of this chapter. An HCT/P that is not solely regulated under section 361 of the Public Health Service Act may be a constituent part of a combination product. Such an HCT/P is subject to part 1271 of this chapter and is also regulated as a drug, device, and/or biological product.

Manufacture includes, but is not limited to, designing, fabricating, assembling, filling, processing, testing, labeling, packaging, repackaging, holding, and storage.

QS regulation refers to the quality system regulation in part 820 of this chapter.

Single-entity combination product has the meaning set forth in § 3.2(e)(1) of this chapter.

Type of constituent part refers to the category of the constituent part, which can be either a biological product, a device, or a drug, as these terms are defined under this section.

§ 4.3 What current good manufacturing practice requirements apply to my combination product?

If you manufacture a combination product, the requirements listed in this section apply as follows:

(a) The current good manufacturing practice requirements in parts 210 and 211 of this chapter apply to a combination product that includes a drug constituent part;

(b) The current good manufacturing practice requirements in part 820 of this chapter apply to a combination product that includes a device constituent part;

(c) The current good manufacturing practice requirements among the requirements (including standards) for biological products in parts 600 through 680 of this chapter apply to a combination product that includes a biological product constituent part to which those requirements would apply if that constituent part were not part of a combination product; and

(d) The current good tissue practice requirements including donor eligibility requirements for HCT/Ps in part 1271 of this chapter apply to a combination product that includes an HCT/P.

§ 4.4 How can I comply with these current good manufacturing practice requirements for a co-packaged or single-entity combination product?

(a) Under this subpart, for single entity or co-packaged combination products, compliance with all applicable current good manufacturing practice requirements for the combination product shall be achieved through the design and implementation of a current good manufacturing practice operating system that is demonstrated to comply with:

(1) The specifics of each set of current good manufacturing practice regulations listed under § 4.3 as they apply to each constituent part included in the combination product; or

(2) Paragraph (b) of this section.

(b) If you elect to establish a current good manufacturing practice operating system in accordance with paragraph (b) of this section, the following requirements apply:

(1) If the combination product includes a device constituent part and a drug constituent part, and the current good manufacturing practice operating system has been shown to comply with the drug CGMPs, the following provisions of the QS regulation must also be shown to have been satisfied; upon demonstration that these requirements have been satisfied, no additional showing of compliance with respect to the QS regulation need be made:

(i) Section 820.20 of this chapter. Management responsibility.

(ii) Section 820.30 of this chapter. Design controls.

(iii) Section 820.50 of this chapter. Purchasing controls.

(iv) Section 820.100 of this chapter. Corrective and preventive action.

(v) Section 820.170 of this chapter. Installation.

(vi) Section 820.200 of this chapter. Servicing.

(2) If the combination product includes a device constituent part and a drug constituent part, and the current good manufacturing practice operating system has been shown to comply with the QS regulation, the following provisions of the drug CGMPs must also be shown to have been satisfied; upon demonstration that these requirements have been satisfied, no additional showing of compliance with respect to the drug CGMPs need be made:

(i) Section 211.84 of this chapter. Testing and approval or rejection of components, drug product containers, and closures.

(ii) Section 211.103 of this chapter. Calculation of yield.

(iii) Section 211.132 of this chapter. Tamper-evident packaging requirements for over-the-counter (OTC) human drug products.

(iv) Section 211.137 of this chapter. Expiration dating.

(v) Section 211.165 of this chapter. Testing and release for distribution.

(vi) Section 211.166 of this chapter. Stability testing.

(vii) Section 211.167 of this chapter. Special testing requirements.

(viii) Section 211.170 of this chapter. Reserve samples.

(3) In addition to being shown to comply with the other applicable manufacturing requirements listed under § 4.3, if the combination product includes a biological product

constituent part, the current good manufacturing practice operating system must also be shown to implement and comply with all manufacturing requirements identified under § 4.3(c) that would apply to that biological product if that constituent part were not part of a combination product.

(4) In addition to being shown to comply with the other applicable current good manufacturing practice requirements listed under § 4.3, if the combination product includes an HCT/P, the current good manufacturing practice operating system must also be shown to implement and comply with all current good tissue practice requirements identified under § 4.3(d) that would apply to that HCT/P if it were not part of a combination product.

(c) During any period in which the manufacture of a constituent part to be included in a co-packaged or single entity combination product occurs at a separate facility from the other constituent part(s) to be included in that single-entity or co-packaged combination product, the current good manufacturing practice operating system for that constituent part at that facility must be demonstrated to comply with all current good manufacturing practice requirements applicable to that type of constituent part.

(d) When two or more types of constituent parts to be included in a single-entity or co-packaged combination product have arrived at the same facility, or the manufacture of these constituent parts is proceeding at the same facility, application of a current good manufacturing process operating system that complies with paragraph (b) of this section may begin.

(e) The requirements set forth in this subpart and in parts 210, 211, 820, 600 through 680, and 1271 of this chapter listed in § 4.3, supplement, and do not supersede, each other unless the regulations explicitly provide otherwise. In the event of a conflict between regulations applicable under this subpart to combination products, including their constituent parts, the regulations most specifically applicable to the constituent part in question shall supersede the more general.

SUBPART B - POSTMARKETING SAFETY REPORTING FOR COMBINATION PRODUCTS

Source: 81 FR 92624, Dec. 20, 2016, unless otherwise noted.

§ 4.100 What is the scope of this subpart?

(a) This subpart identifies postmarketing safety reporting requirements for combination product applicants and constituent part applicants.

(b) This subpart does not apply to investigational combination products, combination products that have not received marketing authorization, or to persons other than combination product applicants and constituent part applicants.

(c) This subpart supplements and does not supersede other provisions of this chapter, including the provisions in parts 314, 600, 606, 803, and 806 of this chapter, unless a regulation explicitly provides otherwise.

§ 4.101 How does the FDA define key terms and phrases in this subpart?

Abbreviated new drug application (ANDA) has the same meaning given the term "abbreviated application" in § 314.3(b) of this chapter.

Agency or we means Food and Drug Administration.

Applicant means, for the purposes of this subpart, a person holding an application under which a combination product or constituent part of a combination product has received marketing authorization (such as approval, licensure, or clearance). For the purposes of this subpart, applicant is used interchangeably with the term "you."

Application means, for purposes of this subpart, a BLA, an NDA, an ANDA, or a device application, including all amendments and supplements to them.

Biological product has the meaning given the term in section 351 of the Public Health Service Act (42 U.S.C. 262).

Biological product deviation report (BPDR) is a report as described in §§ 600.14 and 606.171 of this chapter.

Biologics license application (BLA) has the meaning given the term in section 351 of the Public Health Service Act (42 U.S.C. 262) and § 601.2 of this chapter.

Combination product has the meaning given the term in § 3.2(e) of this chapter.

Combination product applicant means an applicant that holds the application(s) for a combination product.

Constituent part has the meaning given the term in § 4.2.

Constituent part applicant means the applicant for a constituent part of a combination product the constituent parts of which are marketed under applications held by different applicants.

Correction or removal report is a report as described in § 806.10 of this chapter.

De novo classification request is a submission requesting *de novo* classification under section 513(f)(2) of the Federal Food, Drug, and Cosmetic Act.

Device has the meaning given the term in section 201(h) of the Federal Food, Drug, and Cosmetic Act.

Device application means a PMA, PDP, premarket notification submission, *de novo* classification request, or HDE.

Drug has the meaning given the term in section 201(g)(1) of the Federal Food, Drug, and Cosmetic Act.

Field alert report is a report as described in § 314.81 of this chapter.

Fifteen-day report is a report required to be submitted within 15 days as described in § 314.80 of this chapter or § 600.80 of this chapter, as well as followup reports to such a report.

Five-day report is a report as described in §§ 803.3 and 803.53 of this chapter, as well as supplemental or followup reports to such a report as described in § 803.56 of this chapter.

Humanitarian device exemption (HDE) has the meaning given the term in § 814.3 of this chapter.

Malfunction report is a report as described in § 803.50 of this chapter as well as supplemental or followup reports to such a report as described in § 803.56 of this chapter.

New drug application (NDA) has the meaning given the term "application" in § 314.3(b) of this chapter.

Premarket approval application (PMA) has the meaning given the term in § 814.3 of this chapter.

Premarket notification submission is a submission as described in § 807.87 of this chapter.

Product Development Protocol (PDP) is a submission as set forth in section 515(f) of the Federal Food, Drug, and Cosmetic Act.

§ 4.102 What reports must you submit to FDA for your combination product or constituent part?

(a) *In general.* If you are a constituent part applicant, the reporting requirements applicable to you that are identified in this section apply to your constituent part, and if you are a combination product applicant, the reporting requirements applicable to you that are identified in this section apply to your combination product as a whole.

(b) *Reporting requirements applicable to both combination product applicants and constituent part applicants.* If you are a combination product applicant or constituent part applicant, you must comply with the reporting requirements identified in paragraphs (b)(1), (b)(2), or (b)(3) of this section for your product based on its application type. If you are a combination product applicant, you are required to submit a report as specified in this paragraph unless you have already submitted a report in accordance with paragraph (c) of this section for the same event that: Includes the information required under the applicable regulations identified in this paragraph, is required to be submitted in the same manner under § 4.104, and meets the deadlines under the applicable regulations identified in this paragraph.

(1) If your combination product or device constituent part received marketing authorization under a device application, you must comply with the requirements for postmarketing safety reporting described in parts 803 and 806 of this chapter with respect to your product.

(2) If your combination product or drug constituent part received marketing authorization under an NDA or ANDA, you must comply with the requirements for postmarketing safety reporting described in part 314 of this chapter with respect to your product.

(3) If your combination product or biological product constituent part received marketing authorization under a BLA, you must comply with the requirements for postmarketing safety reporting described in parts 600 and 606 of this chapter with respect to your product.

(c) *Reporting requirements applicable only to combination product applicants.* If you are a combination product applicant, in addition to compliance with paragraph (a) of this section, you must also comply with the reporting requirements identified under this paragraph as applicable to your product based on its constituent parts. If you are a combination product applicant, you are required to submit a report as specified in this paragraph unless you have already submitted a report in accordance with paragraph (b) of this section for the same event that: Includes the information required under the applicable regulations for the report identified in this paragraph; is required to be submitted in the same manner under § 4.104 of this chapter; and, unless otherwise specified in this paragraph, meets the deadlines under the applicable regulations for the report identified in this paragraph.

(1) If your combination product contains a device constituent part, you must submit:

(i) Five-day reports;

(ii) Malfunction reports; and

(iii) Correction or removal reports, and maintain records as described in § 806.20 of this chapter for corrections and removals not required to be reported.

(2) If your combination product contains a drug constituent part, you must submit:

(i) Field alert reports; and

(ii) Fifteen-day reports as described in § 314.80 of this chapter, which must be submitted within 30 calendar days instead of 15 calendar days if your combination product received marketing authorization under a device application.

(3) If your combination product contains a biological product constituent part, you must submit:

(i) Biological product deviation reports; and

(ii) Fifteen-day reports as described in § 600.80 of this chapter, which must be submitted within 30 calendar days instead of 15 calendar days if your combination product received marketing authorization under a device application.

(d) *Other reporting requirements for combination product applicants.*

(1) If you are the combination product applicant for a combination product that contains a device constituent part and that received marketing authorization under an NDA, ANDA, or BLA, in addition to the information otherwise required in the periodic safety reports you submit under § 314.80 or § 600.80 of this chapter, your periodic safety reports must also include a summary and analysis of the reports identified in paragraphs (c)(1)(i) and (ii) of this section that were submitted during the report interval.

(2) If you are the combination product applicant for a combination product that received marketing authorization under a device application, in addition to the

reports required under paragraphs (b) and (c) of this section, you must submit reports regarding postmarketing safety events if notified by the Agency in writing that the Agency requires additional information. We will specify what safety information is needed and will require such information if we determine that protection of the public health requires additional or clarifying safety information for the combination product. In any request under this section, we will state the reason or purpose for the safety information request, specify the due date for submitting the information, and clearly identify the reported event(s) related to our request.

§ 4.103 What information must you share with other constituent part applicants for the combination product?

(a) When you receive information regarding an event that involves a death or serious injury as described in § 803.3 of this chapter, or an adverse experience as described in § 314.80(a) of this chapter or § 600.80(a) of this chapter, associated with the use of the combination product, you must provide the information to the other constituent part applicant(s) for the combination product no later than 5 calendar days of your receipt of the information.

(b) With regard to information you must provide to the other constituent part applicant(s) for the combination product, you must maintain records that include:

(1) A copy of the information you provided,

(2) The date the information was received by you,

(3) The date the information was provided to the other constituent part applicant(s), and

(4) The name and address of the other constituent part applicant(s) to whom you provided the information.

§ 4.104 How and where must you submit postmarketing safety reports for your combination product or constituent part?

(a) If you are a constituent part applicant, you must submit postmarketing safety reports in accordance with the regulations identified in § 4.102(b) that are applicable to your product based on its application type.

(b) If you are a combination product applicant, you must submit postmarketing safety reports required under § 4.102 in the manner specified in the regulation applicable to the type of report, with the following exceptions:

(1) You must submit the postmarketing safety reports identified in § 4.102(c)(1)(i) and (ii) in accordance with § 314.80(g) of this chapter if your combination product received marketing authorization under an NDA or ANDA or in accordance with § 600.80(h) of this chapter if your combination product received marketing authorization under a BLA.

(2) You must submit the postmarketing safety reports identified in § 4.102(c)(2)(ii) and (c)(3)(ii) in accordance with § 803.12(a) of this chapter if your combination product received marketing authorization under a device application.

§ 4.105 What are the postmarketing safety reporting recordkeeping requirements for your combination product or constituent part?

(a) If you are a constituent part applicant:

(1) You must maintain records in accordance with the recordkeeping requirements in the applicable regulation(s) described in § 4.102(b).

(2) You must maintain records required under § 4.103(b) for the longest time period required for records under the postmarketing safety reporting regulations applicable to your product under § 4.102(b).

(b) If you are a combination product applicant, you must maintain records in accordance with the longest time period required for records under the regulations applicable to your product under § 4.102.

TITLE 21
FOOD AND DRUGS

CHAPTER I
FOOD AND DRUG ADMINISTRATION, DEPARTMENT OF HEALTH AND HUMAN SERVICES

SUBCHAPTER C – DRUGS: GENERAL

PART 210
CURRENT GOOD MANUFACTURING PRACTICE IN MANUFACTURING, PROCESSING, PACKING, OR HOLDING OF DRUGS; GENERAL

Subpart A - Current Good Manufacturing Practice Requirements for Combination Products
- § 210.1 Status of current good manufacturing practice regulations.
- § 210.1 Applicability of current good manufacturing practice regulations.
- § 210.3 Definitions.

Authority: 21 U.S.C. 321, 351, 352, 355, 360b, 371, 374; 42 U.S.C. 216, 262, 263a, 264.

Source: 43 FR 45076, Sept. 29, 1978, unless otherwise noted.

§ 210.1 Status of current good manufacturing practice regulations.

(a) The regulations set forth in this part and in parts 211, 225, and 226 of this chapter contain the minimum current good manufacturing practice for methods to be used in, and the facilities or controls to be used for, the manufacture, processing, packing, or holding of a drug to assure that such drug meets the requirements of the act as to safety, and has the identity and strength and meets the quality and purity characteristics that it purports or is represented to possess.

(b) The failure to comply with any regulation set forth in this part and in parts 211, 225, and 226 of this chapter in the manufacture, processing, packing, or holding of a drug shall render such drug to be adulterated under section 501(a)(2)(B) of the act and such drug, as well as the person who is responsible for the failure to comply, shall be subject to regulatory action.

(c) Owners and operators of establishments engaged in the recovery, donor screening, testing (including donor testing), processing, storage, labeling, packaging, or distribution of human cells, tissues, and cellular and tissue-based products (HCT/Ps), as defined in § 1271.3(d) of this chapter, that are drugs (subject to review under an application submitted under section 505 of the act or under a biological product license application under section 351 of the Public Health Service Act), are subject to the donor-eligibility and applicable current good tissue practice procedures set forth in part 1271 subparts C and D of this chapter, in addition to the regulations in this part and in parts 211, 225, and 226 of this chapter. Failure to comply with any applicable regulation set forth in this part, in parts 211, 225, and 226 of this chapter, in part 1271 subpart C of this chapter, or in part 1271 subpart D of this chapter with respect to the manufacture, processing, packing or holding of a drug, renders an HCT/P adulterated under section 501(a)(2)(B) of the act. Such HCT/P, as well as the person who is responsible for the failure to comply, is subject to regulatory action.

[43 FR 45076, Sept. 29, 1978, as amended at 69 FR 29828, May 25, 2004; 74 FR 65431, Dec. 10, 2009]

§ 210.2 Applicability of current good manufacturing practice regulations.

(a) The regulations in this part and in parts 211, 225, and 226 of this chapter as they may pertain to a drug; in parts 600 through 680 of this chapter as they may pertain to a biological product for human use; and in part 1271 of this chapter as they are applicable to a human cell, tissue, or cellular or tissue-based product (HCT/P) that is a drug (subject to review under an application submitted under section 505 of the act or under a biological product license application under section 351 of the Public Health Service Act); shall be considered to supplement, not supersede, each other, unless the regulations explicitly provide otherwise. In the event of a conflict between applicable regulations in this part and in other parts of this chapter, the regulation specifically applicable to the drug product in question shall supersede the more general.

(b) If a person engages in only some operations subject to the regulations in this part, in parts 211, 225, and 226 of this chapter, in parts 600 through 680 of this chapter, and in part 1271 of this chapter, and not in others, that person need only comply with those regulations applicable to the operations in which he or she is engaged.

(c) An investigational drug for use in a phase 1 study, as described in § 312.21(a) of this chapter, is subject to the statutory requirements set forth in 21 U.S.C. 351(a)(2)(B). The production of such drug is exempt from compliance with the regulations in part 211 of this chapter. However, this exemption does not apply to an investigational drug for use in a phase 1 study once the investigational drug has been made available for use by or for the sponsor in a phase 2 or phase 3 study, as described in § 312.21(b) and (c) of this chapter, or the drug has been lawfully marketed. If the investigational drug has been made available in a phase 2 or phase 3 study or the drug has been lawfully marketed, the drug for use in the phase 1 study must comply with part 211.

[69 FR 29828, May 25, 2004, as amended at 73 FR 40462, July 15, 2008; 74 FR 65431, Dec. 10, 2009]

§ 210.3 Definitions.

(a) The definitions and interpretations contained in section 201 of the act shall be applicable to such terms when used in this part and in parts 211, 225, and 226 of this chapter.

(b) The following definitions of terms apply to this part and to parts 211, 225, and 226 of this chapter.

(1) *Act* means the Federal Food, Drug, and Cosmetic Act, as amended (21 U.S.C. 301 *et seq.*).

(2) **Batch** means a specific quantity of a drug or other material that is intended to have uniform character and quality, within specified limits, and is produced according

to a single manufacturing order during the same cycle of manufacture.

(3) ***Component*** means any ingredient intended for use in the manufacture of a drug product, including those that may not appear in such drug product.

(4) ***Drug product*** means a finished dosage form, for example, tablet, capsule, solution, etc., that contains an active drug ingredient generally, but not necessarily, in association with inactive ingredients. The term also includes a finished dosage form that does not contain an active ingredient but is intended to be used as a placebo.

(5) ***Fiber*** means any particulate contaminant with a length at least three times greater than its width.

(6) ***Nonfiber releasing filter*** means any filter, which after appropriate pretreatment such as washing or flushing, will not release fibers into the component or drug product that is being filtered.

(7) ***Active ingredient*** means any component that is intended to furnish pharmacological activity or other direct effect in the diagnosis, cure, mitigation, treatment, or prevention of disease, or to affect the structure or any function of the body of man or other animals. The term includes those components that may undergo chemical change in the manufacture of the drug product and be present in the drug product in a modified form intended to furnish the specified activity or effect.

(8) *Inactive ingredient* means any component other than an *active ingredient*.

(9) *In-process material* means any material fabricated, compounded, blended, or derived by chemical reaction that is produced for, and used in, the preparation of the drug product.

(10) *Lot* means a batch, or a specific identified portion of a batch, having uniform character and quality within specified limits; or, in the case of a drug product produced by continuous process, it is a specific identified amount produced in a unit of time or quantity in a manner that assures its having uniform character and quality within specified limits.

(11) *Lot number, control number, or batch number* means any distinctive combination of letters, numbers, or symbols, or any combination of them, from which the complete history of the manufacture, processing, packing, holding, and distribution of a batch or lot of drug product or other material can be determined.

(12) *Manufacture, processing, packing, or holding of a drug product* includes packaging and labeling operations, testing, and quality control of drug products.

(13) The term *medicated feed* means any Type B or Type C medicated feed as defined in § 558.3 of this chapter. The feed contains one or more drugs as defined in section 201(g) of the act. The manufacture of medicated feeds is subject to the requirements of part 225 of this chapter.

(14) The term *medicated premix* means a Type A medicated article as defined in § 558.3 of this chapter. The article contains one or more drugs as defined in section 201(g) of the act. The manufacture of medicated premixes is subject to the requirements of part 226 of this chapter.

(15) *Quality control unit* means any person or organizational element designated by the firm to be responsible for the duties relating to quality control.

(16) *Strength* means:

(i) The concentration of the drug substance (for example, weight/weight, weight/volume, or unit dose/volume basis), and/or

(ii) The potency, that is, the therapeutic activity of the drug product as indicated by appropriate laboratory tests or by adequately developed and controlled clinical data (expressed, for example, in terms of units by reference to a standard).

(17) *Theoretical yield* means the quantity that would be produced at any appropriate phase of manufacture, processing, or packing of a particular drug product, based upon the quantity of components to be used, in the absence of any loss or error in actual production.

(18) *Actual yield* means the quantity that is actually produced at any appropriate phase of manufacture, processing, or packing of a particular drug product.

(19) *Percentage of theoretical yield* means the ratio of the actual yield (at any appropriate phase of manufacture,

processing, or packing of a particular drug product) to the theoretical yield (at the same phase), stated as a percentage.

(20) *Acceptance criteria* means the product specifications and acceptance/rejection criteria, such as acceptable quality level and unacceptable quality level, with an associated sampling plan, that are necessary for making a decision to accept or reject a lot or batch (or any other convenient subgroups of manufactured units).

(21) *Representative sample* means a sample that consists of a number of units that are drawn based on rational criteria such as random sampling and intended to assure that the sample accurately portrays the material being sampled.

(22) Gang-printed labeling means labeling derived from a sheet of material on which more than one item of labeling is printed.

[43 FR 45076, Sept. 29, 1978, as amended at 51 FR 7389, Mar. 3, 1986; 58 FR 41353, Aug. 3, 1993; 73 FR 51931, Sept. 8, 2008; 74 FR 65431, Dec. 10, 2009]

TITLE 21
FOOD AND DRUGS

CHAPTER I
FOOD AND DRUG ADMINISTRATION, DEPARTMENT OF HEALTH AND HUMAN SERVICES

SUBCHAPTER C – DRUGS: GENERAL

PART 211
CURRENT GOOD MANUFACTURING PRACTICE FOR FINISHED PHARMACEUTICALS

Subpart A - General Provisions
§ 211.1 Scope.
Subpart B - Organization and Personnel
§ 211.22 Responsibilities of quality control unit.
§ 211.25 Personnel qualifications.
§ 211.28 Personnel responsibilities.
§ 211.34 Consultants.
Subpart C - Buildings and Facilities
§ 211.42 Design and construction features.
§ 211.44 Lighting.
§ 211.46 Ventilation, air filtration, air heating and cooling.
§ 211.48 Plumbing.
§ 211.50 Sewage and refuse.
§ 211.52 Washing and toilet facilities.
§ 211.56 Sanitation.
§ 211.58 Maintenance.

Subpart D - Equipment
§ 211.63 Equipment design, size, and location.
§ 211.65 Equipment construction.
§ 211.67 Equipment cleaning and maintenance.
§ 211.68 Automatic, mechanical, and electronic equipment.
§ 211.72 Filters.

Subpart E - Control of Components and Drug Product Containers and Closures
§ 211.80 General requirements.
§ 211.82 Receipt and storage of untested components, drug product containers, and closures.
§ 211.84 Testing and approval or rejection of components, drug product containers, and closures.
§ 211.86 Use of approved components, drug product containers, and closures.
§ 211.87 Retesting of approved components, drug product containers, and closures.
§ 211.89 Rejected components, drug product containers, and closures.
§ 211.94 Drug product containers and closures.

Subpart F- Production and Process Controls
§ 211.100 Written procedures; deviations.
§ 211.101 Charge-in of components.
§ 211.103 Calculation of yield.
§ 211.105 Equipment identification.
§ 211.110 Sampling and testing of in-process materials and drug products.
§ 211.111 Time limitations on production.

§ 211.113 Control of microbiological contamination.
§ 211.115 Reprocessing.

Subpart G - Packaging and Labeling Control

§ 211.122 Materials examination and usage criteria.
§ 211.125 Labeling issuance.
§ 211.130 Packaging and labeling operations.
§ 211.132 Tamper-evident packaging requirements for over-the-counter (OTC) human drug products.
§ 211.134 Drug product inspection.
§ 211.137 Expiration dating.

Subpart H - Holding and Distribution

§ 211.142 Warehousing procedures.
§ 211.150 Distribution procedures.

Subpart I - Laboratory Controls

§ 211.160 General requirements.
§ 211.165 Testing and release for distribution.
§ 211.166 Stability testing.
§ 211.167 Special testing requirements.
§ 211.170 Reserve samples.
§ 211.173 Laboratory animals.
§ 211.176 Penicillin contamination.

Subpart J - Records and Reports

§ 211.180 General requirements.
§ 211.182 Equipment cleaning and use log.
§ 211.184 Component, drug product container, closure, and labeling records.
§ 211.186 Master production and control records.
§ 211.188 Batch production and control records.
§ 211.192 Production record review.

§ 211.194   Laboratory records.
§ 211.196   Distribution records.
§ 211.198   Complaint files.

Subpart K - Returned and Salvaged Drug Products

§ 211.204   Returned drug products.
§ 211.208   Drug product salvaging.

Authority: 21 U.S.C. 321, 351, 352, 355, 360b, 371, 374; 42 U.S.C. 216, 262, 263a, 264.

Source: 43 FR 45077, Sept. 29, 1978, unless otherwise noted.

Subpart A - General Provisions

§ 211.1 Scope.

(a) The regulations in this part contain the minimum current good manufacturing practice for preparation of drug products (excluding positron emission tomography drugs) for administration to humans or animals.

(b) The current good manufacturing practice regulations in this chapter as they pertain to drug products; in parts 600 through 680 of this chapter, as they pertain to drugs that are also biological products for human use; and in part 1271 of this chapter, as they are applicable to drugs that are also human cells, tissues, and cellular and tissue-based products (HCT/Ps) and that are drugs (subject to review under an application submitted under section 505 of the act or under a biological product license application under section 351 of the Public Health Service Act); supplement and do not supersede the regulations in this part unless the regulations explicitly provide otherwise. In the event of a conflict between applicable regulations in this part and in other parts of this chapter, or in parts 600 through 680 of this chapter, or in part 1271 of this chapter, the regulation specifically applicable to the drug product in question shall supersede the more general.

(c) Pending consideration of a proposed exemption, published in the Federal Register of September 29, 1978, the requirements in this part shall not be enforced for OTC drug products if the products and all their ingredients are ordinarily marketed and consumed as human foods, and which products may also fall within the legal definition of drugs by virtue of their intended use. Therefore, until further notice, regulations under parts 110 and 117 of this chapter, and where applicable, parts 113 through 129 of this chapter, shall be applied in determining whether these OTC drug products that are also foods are manufactured, processed, packed, or held under current good manufacturing practice.

[43 FR 45077, Sept. 29, 1978, as amended at 62 FR 66522, Dec. 19, 1997; 69 FR 29828, May 25, 2004; 74 FR 65431, Dec. 10, 2009; 80 FR 56168, Sept. 17, 2015]

§ 211.3 Definitions.

The definitions set forth in § 210.3 of this chapter apply in this part.

SUBPART B - ORGANIZATION AND PERSONNEL

§ 211.22 Responsibilities of quality control unit.

(a) There shall be a quality control unit that shall have the responsibility and authority to approve or reject all components, drug product containers, closures, in-process materials, packaging material, labeling, and drug products, and the authority to review production records to assure that no errors have occurred or, if errors have occurred, that they have been fully investigated. The quality control unit shall be responsible for approving or rejecting drug products manufactured, processed, packed, or held under contract by another company.

(b) Adequate laboratory facilities for the testing and approval (or rejection) of components, drug product containers, closures, packaging materials, in-process materials, and drug products shall be available to the quality control unit.

(c) The quality control unit shall have the responsibility for approving or rejecting all procedures or specifications impacting on the identity, strength, quality, and purity of the drug product.

(d) The responsibilities and procedures applicable to the quality control unit shall be in writing; such written procedures shall be followed.

§ 211.25 Personnel qualifications.

(a) Each person engaged in the manufacture, processing, packing, or holding of a drug product shall have education, training, and experience, or any combination thereof, to enable that person to perform the assigned functions. Training shall be in the particular operations that the employee performs and in current good manufacturing practice (including the current good manufacturing practice regulations in this chapter and written procedures required by these regulations) as they relate to the employee's functions. Training in current good manufacturing practice shall be conducted by qualified individuals on a continuing basis and with sufficient frequency to assure that employees remain familiar with CGMP requirements applicable to them.

(b) Each person responsible for supervising the manufacture, processing, packing, or holding of a drug product shall have the education, training, and experience, or any combination thereof, to perform assigned functions in such a manner as to provide assurance that the drug product has the safety, identity, strength, quality, and purity that it purports or is represented to possess.

(c) There shall be an adequate number of qualified personnel to perform and supervise the manufacture, processing, packing, or holding of each drug product.

§ 211.28 Personnel responsibilities.

(a) Personnel engaged in the manufacture, processing, packing, or holding of a drug product shall wear clean clothing appropriate for the duties they perform. Protective apparel, such as head, face, hand, and arm coverings, shall be worn as necessary to protect drug products from contamination.

(b) Personnel shall practice good sanitation and health habits.

(c) Only personnel authorized by supervisory personnel shall enter those areas of the buildings and facilities designated as limited-access areas.

(d) Any person shown at any time (either by medical examination or supervisory observation) to have an apparent illness or open lesions that may adversely affect the safety or quality of drug products shall be excluded from direct contact with components, drug product containers, closures, in-process materials, and drug products until the condition is corrected or determined by competent medical personnel not to jeopardize the safety or quality of drug products. All personnel shall be instructed to report to supervisory personnel any health conditions that may have an adverse effect on drug products.

§ 211.34 Consultants.

Consultants advising on the manufacture, processing, packing, or holding of drug products shall have sufficient education, training, and experience, or any combination thereof, to advise on the subject for which they are retained. Records shall be maintained stating the name, address, and qualifications of any consultants and the type of service they provide.

SUBPART C - BUILDINGS AND FACILITIES

§ 211.42 Design and construction features.

(a) Any building or buildings used in the manufacture, processing, packing, or holding of a drug product shall be of suitable size, construction and location to facilitate cleaning, maintenance, and proper operations.

(b) Any such building shall have adequate space for the orderly placement of equipment and materials to prevent mixups between different components, drug product containers, closures, labeling, in-process materials, or drug products, and to prevent contamination. The flow of components, drug product containers, closures, labeling, in-process materials, and drug products through the building or buildings shall be designed to prevent contamination.

(c) Operations shall be performed within specifically defined areas of adequate size. There shall be separate or defined areas or such other control systems for the firm's operations as are necessary to prevent contamination or mixups during the course of the following procedures:

(1) Receipt, identification, storage, and withholding from use of components, drug product containers, closures, and labeling, pending the appropriate sampling, testing, or examination by the quality control unit before release for manufacturing or packaging;

(2) Holding rejected components, drug product containers, closures, and labeling before disposition;

(3) Storage of released components, drug product containers, closures, and labeling;

(4) Storage of in-process materials;

(5) Manufacturing and processing operations;

(6) Packaging and labeling operations;

(7) Quarantine storage before release of drug products;

(8) Storage of drug products after release;

(9) Control and laboratory operations;

(10) Aseptic processing, which includes as appropriate:

(i) Floors, walls, and ceilings of smooth, hard surfaces that are easily cleanable;

(ii) Temperature and humidity controls;

(iii) An air supply filtered through high-efficiency particulate air filters under positive pressure, regardless of whether flow is laminar or nonlaminar;

(iv) A system for monitoring environmental conditions;

(v) A system for cleaning and disinfecting the room and equipment to produce aseptic conditions;

(vi) A system for maintaining any equipment used to control the aseptic conditions.

(d) Operations relating to the manufacture, processing, and packing of penicillin shall be performed in facilities separate from those used for other drug products for human use.

[43 FR 45077, Sept. 29, 1978, as amended at 60 FR 4091, Jan. 20, 1995]

§ 211.44 Lighting.

Adequate lighting shall be provided in all areas.

§ 211.46 Ventilation, air filtration, air heating and cooling.

(a) Adequate ventilation shall be provided.

(b) Equipment for adequate control over air pressure, micro-organisms, dust, humidity, and temperature shall be provided when appropriate for the manufacture, processing, packing, or holding of a drug product.

(c) Air filtration systems, including prefilters and particulate matter air filters, shall be used when appropriate on air supplies to production areas. If air is recirculated to production areas, measures shall be taken to control recirculation of dust from production. In areas where air contamination occurs during production, there shall be adequate exhaust systems or other systems adequate to control contaminants.

(d) Air-handling systems for the manufacture, processing, and packing of penicillin shall be completely separate from those for other drug products for human use.

§ 211.48 Plumbing.

(a) Potable water shall be supplied under continuous positive pressure in a plumbing system free of defects that could contribute contamination to any drug product. Potable water shall meet the standards prescribed in the Environmental Protection Agency's Primary Drinking

Water Regulations set forth in 40 CFR part 141. Water not meeting such standards shall not be permitted in the potable water system.

(b) Drains shall be of adequate size and, where connected directly to a sewer, shall be provided with an air break or other mechanical device to prevent back-siphonage.

[43 FR 45077, Sept. 29, 1978, as amended at 48 FR 11426, Mar. 18, 1983]

§ 211.50 Sewage and refuse.

Sewage, trash, and other refuse in and from the building and immediate premises shall be disposed of in a safe and sanitary manner.

§ 211.52 Washing and toilet facilities.

Adequate washing facilities shall be provided, including hot and cold water, soap or detergent, air driers or single-service towels, and clean toilet facilities easily accessible to working areas.

§ 211.56 Sanitation.

(a) Any building used in the manufacture, processing, packing, or holding of a drug product shall be maintained in a clean and sanitary condition, Any such building shall be free of infestation by rodents, birds, insects, and other vermin (other than laboratory animals). Trash and organic waste matter shall be held and disposed of in a timely and sanitary manner.

(b) There shall be written procedures assigning responsibility for sanitation and describing in sufficient detail the cleaning schedules, methods, equipment, and materials to be used in cleaning the buildings and facilities; such written procedures shall be followed.

(c) There shall be written procedures for use of suitable rodenticides, insecticides, fungicides, fumigating agents, and cleaning and sanitizing agents. Such written procedures shall be designed to prevent the contamination of equipment, components, drug product containers, closures, packaging, labeling materials, or drug products and shall be followed. Rodenticides, insecticides, and fungicides shall not be used unless registered and used in accordance with the Federal Insecticide, Fungicide, and Rodenticide Act (7 U.S.C. 135).

(d) Sanitation procedures shall apply to work performed by contractors or temporary employees as well as work performed by full-time employees during the ordinary course of operations.

§ 211.58 Maintenance.

Any building used in the manufacture, processing, packing, or holding of a drug product shall be maintained in a good state of repair.

SUBPART D - EQUIPMENT

§ 211.63 Equipment design, size, and location.

Equipment used in the manufacture, processing, packing, or holding of a drug product shall be of appropriate design, adequate size, and suitably located to facilitate operations for its intended use and for its cleaning and maintenance.

§ 211.65 Equipment construction.

(a) Equipment shall be constructed so that surfaces that contact components, in-process materials, or drug products shall not be reactive, additive, or absorptive so as to alter the safety, identity, strength, quality, or purity of the drug product beyond the official or other established requirements.

(b) Any substances required for operation, such as lubricants or coolants, shall not come into contact with components, drug product containers, closures, in-process materials, or drug products so as to alter the safety, identity, strength, quality, or purity of the drug product beyond the official or other established requirements.

§ 211.67 Equipment cleaning and maintenance.

(a) Equipment and utensils shall be cleaned, maintained, and, as appropriate for the nature of the drug, sanitized and/or sterilized at appropriate intervals to prevent malfunctions or contamination that would alter the safety, identity, strength, quality, or purity of the drug product beyond the official or other established requirements.

(b) Written procedures shall be established and followed for cleaning and maintenance of equipment, including utensils, used in the manufacture, processing, packing, or holding of a drug product. These procedures shall include, but are not necessarily limited to, the following:

(1) Assignment of responsibility for cleaning and maintaining equipment;

(2) Maintenance and cleaning schedules, including, where appropriate, sanitizing schedules;

(3) A description in sufficient detail of the methods, equipment, and materials used in cleaning and maintenance operations, and the methods of disassembling and reassembling equipment as necessary to assure proper cleaning and maintenance;

(4) Removal or obliteration of previous batch identification;

(5) Protection of clean equipment from contamination prior to use;

(6) Inspection of equipment for cleanliness immediately before use.

(c) Records shall be kept of maintenance, cleaning, sanitizing, and inspection as specified in §§ 211.180 and 211.182.

[43 FR 45077, Sept. 29, 1978, as amended at 73 FR 51931, Sept. 8, 2008]

§ 211.68 Automatic, mechanical, and electronic equipment.

(a) Automatic, mechanical, or electronic equipment or other types of equipment, including computers, or related systems that will perform a function satisfactorily, may be used in the manufacture, processing, packing, and holding of a drug product. If such equipment is so used, it shall be routinely calibrated, inspected, or checked according to a written program designed to assure proper performance. Written records of those calibration checks and inspections shall be maintained.

(b) Appropriate controls shall be exercised over computer or related systems to assure that changes in master production and control records or other records are instituted only by authorized personnel. Input to and output from the computer or related system of formulas or other records or data shall be checked for accuracy. The degree and frequency of input/output verification shall be based on the complexity and reliability of the computer or related system. A backup file of data entered into the computer or related system shall be maintained except where certain data, such as calculations performed in connection with laboratory analysis, are eliminated by computerization or other automated processes. In such instances a written record of the program shall be maintained along with appropriate validation data. Hard copy or alternative systems, such as duplicates, tapes, or microfilm, designed to assure that backup data are exact and complete and that it is secure from alteration, inadvertent erasures, or loss shall be maintained.

(c) Such automated equipment used for performance of operations addressed by §§ 211.101(c) or (d), 211.103, 211.182, or 211.188(b)(11) can satisfy the requirements included in those sections relating to the performance of an operation by one person and checking by another person if such equipment is used in conformity with this section, and one person checks that the equipment properly performed the operation.

[43 FR 45077, Sept. 29, 1978, as amended at 60 FR 4091, Jan. 20, 1995; 73 FR 51932, Sept. 8, 2008]

§ 211.72 Filters.

Filters for liquid filtration used in the manufacture, processing, or packing of injectable drug products intended for human use shall not release fibers into such products. Fiber-releasing filters may be used when it is not possible to manufacture such products without the use of these filters. If use of a fiber-releasing filter is necessary, an additional nonfiber-releasing filter having a maximum nominal pore size rating of 0.2 micron (0.45 micron if the manufacturing conditions so dictate) shall subsequently be used to reduce the content of particles in the injectable drug product. The use of an asbestos-containing filter is prohibited.

[73 FR 51932, Sept. 8, 2008]

SUBPART E - CONTROL OF COMPONENTS AND DRUG PRODUCT CONTAINERS AND CLOSURES

§ 211.80 General requirements.

(a) There shall be written procedures describing in sufficient detail the receipt, identification, storage, handling, sampling, testing, and approval or rejection of components and drug product containers and closures; such written procedures shall be followed.

(b) Components and drug product containers and closures shall at all times be handled and stored in a manner to prevent contamination.

(c) Bagged or boxed components of drug product containers, or closures shall be stored off the floor and suitably spaced to permit cleaning and inspection.

(d) Each container or grouping of containers for components or drug product containers, or closures shall be identified with a distinctive code for each lot in each shipment received. This code shall be used in recording the disposition of each lot. Each lot shall be appropriately identified as to its status (i.e., quarantined, approved, or rejected).

§ 211.82 Receipt and storage of untested components, drug product containers, and closures.

(a) Upon receipt and before acceptance, each container or grouping of containers of components, drug product containers, and closures shall be examined visually for appropriate labeling as to contents, container damage or broken seals, and contamination.

(b) Components, drug product containers, and closures shall be stored under quarantine until they have been tested or examined, whichever is appropriate, and released. Storage within the area shall conform to the requirements of § 211.80.

[43 FR 45077, Sept. 29, 1978, as amended at 73 FR 51932, Sept. 8, 2008]

§ 211.84 Testing and approval or rejection of components, drug product containers, and closures.

(a) Each lot of components, drug product containers, and closures shall be withheld from use until the lot has been sampled, tested, or examined, as appropriate, and released for use by the quality control unit.

(b) Representative samples of each shipment of each lot shall be collected for testing or examination. The number of containers to be sampled, and the amount of material to be taken from each container, shall be based upon appropriate criteria such as statistical criteria for component variability, confidence levels, and degree of precision desired, the past quality history of the supplier, and the quantity needed for analysis and reserve where required by § 211.170.

(c) Samples shall be collected in accordance with the following procedures:

(1) The containers of components selected shall be cleaned when necessary in a manner to prevent introduction of contaminants into the component.

(2) The containers shall be opened, sampled, and resealed in a manner designed to prevent contamination of their contents and contamination of other components, drug product containers, or closures.

(3) Sterile equipment and aseptic sampling techniques shall be used when necessary.

(4) If it is necessary to sample a component from the top, middle, and bottom of its container, such sample subdivisions shall not be composited for testing.

(5) Sample containers shall be identified so that the following information can be determined: name of the material sampled, the lot number, the container from which the sample was taken, the date on which the sample was taken, and the name of the person who collected the sample.

(6) Containers from which samples have been taken shall be marked to show that samples have been removed from them.

(d) Samples shall be examined and tested as follows:

(1) At least one test shall be conducted to verify the identity of each component of a drug product. Specific identity tests, if they exist, shall be used.

(2) Each component shall be tested for conformity with all appropriate written specifications for purity, strength, and quality. In lieu of such testing by the manufacturer, a report of analysis may be accepted from the supplier of a component, provided that at least one specific identity test is conducted on such component by the manufacturer, and provided that the manufacturer establishes the reliability of the supplier's analyses through appropriate validation of the supplier's test results at appropriate intervals.

(3) Containers and closures shall be tested for conformity with all appropriate written specifications. In lieu of such

testing by the manufacturer, a certificate of testing may be accepted from the supplier, provided that at least a visual identification is conducted on such containers/closures by the manufacturer and provided that the manufacturer establishes the reliability of the supplier's test results through appropriate validation of the supplier's test results at appropriate intervals.

(4) When appropriate, components shall be microscopically examined.

(5) Each lot of a component, drug product container, or closure that is liable to contamination with filth, insect infestation, or other extraneous adulterant shall be examined against established specifications for such contamination.

(6) Each lot of a component, drug product container, or closure with potential for microbiological contamination that is objectionable in view of its intended use shall be subjected to microbiological tests before use.

(e) Any lot of components, drug product containers, or closures that meets the appropriate written specifications of identity, strength, quality, and purity and related tests under paragraph (d) of this section may be approved and released for use. Any lot of such material that does not meet such specifications shall be rejected.

[43 FR 45077, Sept. 29, 1978, as amended at 63 FR 14356, Mar. 25, 1998; 73 FR 51932, Sept. 8, 2008]

§ 211.86 Use of approved components, drug product containers, and closures.

Components, drug product containers, and closures approved for use shall be rotated so that the oldest approved stock is used first. Deviation from this requirement is permitted if such deviation is temporary and appropriate.

§ 211.87 Retesting of approved components, drug product containers, and closures.

Components, drug product containers, and closures shall be retested or reexamined, as appropriate, for identity, strength, quality, and purity and approved or rejected by the quality control unit in accordance with § 211.84 as necessary, e.g., after storage for long periods or after exposure to air, heat or other conditions that might adversely affect the component, drug product container, or closure.

§ 211.89 Rejected components, drug product containers, and closures.

Rejected components, drug product containers, and closures shall be identified and controlled under a quarantine system designed to prevent their use in manufacturing or processing operations for which they are unsuitable.

§ 211.94 Drug product containers and closures.

(a) Drug product containers and closures shall not be reactive, additive, or absorptive so as to alter the safety, identity, strength, quality, or purity of the drug beyond the official or established requirements.

(b) Container closure systems shall provide adequate protection against foreseeable external factors in storage and use that can cause deterioration or contamination of the drug product.

(c) Drug product containers and closures shall be clean and, where indicated by the nature of the drug, sterilized and processed to remove pyrogenic properties to assure that they are suitable for their intended use. Such depyrogenation processes shall be validated.

(d) Standards or specifications, methods of testing, and, where indicated, methods of cleaning, sterilizing, and processing to remove pyrogenic properties shall be written and followed for drug product containers and closures.

(e) *Medical gas containers and closures must meet the following requirements* -

(1) *Gas-specific use outlet connections.* Portable cryogenic medical gas containers that are not manufactured with permanent gas use outlet connections (*e.g.,* those that have been silver-brazed) must have gas-specific use outlet connections that are attached to the valve body so that they cannot be readily removed or replaced (without making the valve inoperable and preventing the containers' use) except by the manufacturer. For the purposes of this paragraph, the term "manufacturer" includes any individual or firm that fills high-pressure medical gas cylinders or cryogenic medical

gas containers. For the purposes of this section, a "portable cryogenic medical gas container" is one that is capable of being transported and is intended to be attached to a medical gas supply system within a hospital, health care entity, nursing home, other facility, or home health care setting, or is a base unit used to fill small cryogenic gas containers for use by individual patients. The term does not include cryogenic containers that are not designed to be connected to a medical gas supply system, *e.g.,* tank trucks, trailers, rail cars, or small cryogenic gas containers for use by individual patients (including portable liquid oxygen units as defined at § 868.5655 of this chapter).

(2) *Label and coloring requirements.* The labeling specified at § 201.328(a) of this chapter must be affixed to the container in a manner that does not interfere with other labeling and such that it is not susceptible to becoming worn or inadvertently detached during normal use. Each such label as well as materials used for coloring medical gas containers must be reasonably resistant to fading, durable when exposed to atmospheric conditions, and not readily soluble in water.

[43 FR 45077, Sept. 29, 1978, as amended at 73 FR 51932, Sept. 8, 2008; 81 FR 81697, Nov. 18, 2016]

Subpart F - Production and Process Controls

§ 211.100 Written procedures; deviations.

(a) There shall be written procedures for production and process control designed to assure that the drug products have the identity, strength, quality, and purity they purport or are represented to possess. Such procedures shall include all requirements in this subpart. These written procedures, including any changes, shall be drafted, reviewed, and approved by the appropriate organizational units and reviewed and approved by the quality control unit.

(b) Written production and process control procedures shall be followed in the execution of the various production and process control functions and shall be documented at the time of performance. Any deviation from the written procedures shall be recorded and justified.

§ 211.101 Charge-in of components.

Written production and control procedures shall include the following, which are designed to assure that the drug products produced have the identity, strength, quality, and purity they purport or are represented to possess:

(a) The batch shall be formulated with the intent to provide not less than 100 percent of the labeled or established amount of active ingredient.

(b) Components for drug product manufacturing shall be weighed, measured, or subdivided as appropriate. If a component is removed from the original container to another, the new container shall be identified with the following information:

(1) Component name or item code;

(2) Receiving or control number;

(3) Weight or measure in new container;

(4) Batch for which component was dispensed, including its product name, strength, and lot number.

(c) Weighing, measuring, or subdividing operations for components shall be adequately supervised. Each container of component dispensed to manufacturing shall be examined by a second person to assure that:

(1) The component was released by the quality control unit;

(2) The weight or measure is correct as stated in the batch production records;

(3) The containers are properly identified. If the weighing, measuring, or subdividing operations are performed by automated equipment under § 211.68, only one person is needed to assure paragraphs (c)(1), (c)(2), and (c)(3) of this section.

(d) Each component shall either be added to the batch by one person and verified by a second person or, if the components are added by automated equipment under § 211.68, only verified by one person.

[43 FR 45077, Sept. 29, 1978, as amended at 73 FR 51932, Sept. 8, 2008]

§ 211.103 Calculation of yield.

Actual yields and percentages of theoretical yield shall be determined at the conclusion of each appropriate phase of manufacturing, processing, packaging, or holding of the drug product. Such calculations shall either be performed by one person and independently verified by a second person, or, if the yield is calculated by automated equipment under § 211.68, be independently verified by one person.

[73 FR 51932, Sept. 8, 2008]

§ 211.105 Equipment identification.

(a) All compounding and storage containers, processing lines, and major equipment used during the production of a batch of a drug product shall be properly identified at all times to indicate their contents and, when necessary, the phase of processing of the batch.

(b) Major equipment shall be identified by a distinctive identification number or code that shall be recorded in the batch production record to show the specific equipment used in the manufacture of each batch of a drug product. In cases where only one of a particular type of equipment exists in a manufacturing facility, the name of the equipment may be used in lieu of a distinctive identification number or code.

§ 211.110 Sampling and testing of in-process materials and drug products.

(a) To assure batch uniformity and integrity of drug products, written procedures shall be established and followed that describe the in-process controls, and tests, or examinations to be conducted on appropriate samples of in-process materials of each batch. Such control procedures shall be established to monitor the output and to validate the performance of those manufacturing processes that may be responsible for causing variability in the characteristics of in-process material and the drug product. Such control procedures shall include, but are not limited to, the following, where appropriate:

(1) Tablet or capsule weight variation;

(2) Disintegration time;

(3) Adequacy of mixing to assure uniformity and homogeneity;

(4) Dissolution time and rate;

(5) Clarity, completeness, or pH of solutions.

(6) Bioburden testing.

(b) Valid in-process specifications for such characteristics shall be consistent with drug product final specifications and shall be derived from previous acceptable process average and process variability estimates where possible and determined by the application of suitable statistical procedures where appropriate. Examination and testing of samples shall assure that the drug product and in-process material conform to specifications.

(c) In-process materials shall be tested for identity, strength, quality, and purity as appropriate, and approved or rejected by the quality control unit, during the production process, e.g., at commencement or completion of significant phases or after storage for long periods.

(d) Rejected in-process materials shall be identified and controlled under a quarantine system designed to prevent their use in manufacturing or processing operations for which they are unsuitable.

[43 FR 45077, Sept. 29, 1978, as amended at 73 FR 51932, Sept. 8, 2008]

§ 211.111 Time limitations on production.

When appropriate, time limits for the completion of each phase of production shall be established to assure the quality of the drug product. Deviation from established time limits may be acceptable if such deviation does not compromise the quality of the drug product. Such deviation shall be justified and documented.

§ 211.113 Control of microbiological contamination.

(a) Appropriate written procedures, designed to prevent objectionable microorganisms in drug products not required to be sterile, shall be established and followed.

(b) Appropriate written procedures, designed to prevent microbiological contamination of drug products purporting to be sterile, shall be established and followed. Such procedures shall include validation of all aseptic and sterilization processes.

[43 FR 45077, Sept. 29, 1978, as amended at 73 FR 51932, Sept. 8, 2008]

§ 211.115 Reprocessing.

(a) Written procedures shall be established and followed prescribing a system for reprocessing batches that do not conform to standards or specifications and the steps to be taken to insure that the reprocessed batches will conform with all established standards, specifications, and characteristics.

(b) Reprocessing shall not be performed without the review and approval of the quality control unit.

SUBPART G - PACKAGING AND LABELING CONTROL

§ 211.122 Materials examination and usage criteria.

(a) There shall be written procedures describing in sufficient detail the receipt, identification, storage, handling, sampling, examination, and/or testing of labeling and packaging materials; such written procedures shall be followed. Labeling and packaging materials shall be representatively sampled, and examined or tested upon receipt and before use in packaging or labeling of a drug product.

(b) Any labeling or packaging materials meeting appropriate written specifications may be approved and released for use. Any labeling or packaging materials that do not meet such specifications shall be rejected to prevent their use in operations for which they are unsuitable.

(c) Records shall be maintained for each shipment received of each different labeling and packaging material indicating receipt, examination or testing, and whether accepted or rejected.

(d) Labels and other labeling materials for each different drug product, strength, dosage form, or quantity of contents shall be stored separately with suitable identification. Access to the storage area shall be limited to authorized personnel.

(e) Obsolete and outdated labels, labeling, and other packaging materials shall be destroyed.

(f) Use of gang-printed labeling for different drug products, or different strengths or net contents of the same drug product, is prohibited unless the labeling from gang-printed sheets is adequately differentiated by size, shape, or color.

(g) If cut labeling is used for immediate container labels, individual unit cartons, or multiunit cartons containing immediate containers that are not packaged in individual unit cartons, packaging and labeling operations shall include one of the following special control procedures:

(1) Dedication of labeling and packaging lines to each different strength of each different drug product;

(2) Use of appropriate electronic or electromechanical equipment to conduct a 100-percent examination for correct labeling during or after completion of finishing operations; or

(3) Use of visual inspection to conduct a 100-percent examination for correct labeling during or after completion

of finishing operations for hand-applied labeling. Such examination shall be performed by one person and independently verified by a second person.

(4) Use of any automated technique, including differentiation by labeling size and shape, that physically prevents incorrect labeling from being processed by labeling and packaging equipment.

(h) Printing devices on, or associated with, manufacturing lines used to imprint labeling upon the drug product unit label or case shall be monitored to assure that all imprinting conforms to the print specified in the batch production record.

[43 FR 45077, Sept. 29, 1978, as amended at 58 FR 41353, Aug. 3, 1993; 77 FR 16163, Mar. 20, 2012]

§ 211.125 Labeling issuance.

(a) Strict control shall be exercised over labeling issued for use in drug product labeling operations.

(b) Labeling materials issued for a batch shall be carefully examined for identity and conformity to the labeling specified in the master or batch production records.

(c) Procedures shall be used to reconcile the quantities of labeling issued, used, and returned, and shall require evaluation of discrepancies found between the quantity of drug product finished and the quantity of labeling issued when such discrepancies are outside narrow preset limits based on historical operating data. Such discrepancies shall be investigated in accordance with § 211.192.

Labeling reconciliation is waived for cut or roll labeling if a 100-percent examination for correct labeling is performed in accordance with § 211.122(g)(2). Labeling reconciliation is also waived for 360° wraparound labels on portable cryogenic medical gas containers.

(d) All excess labeling bearing lot or control numbers shall be destroyed.

(e) Returned labeling shall be maintained and stored in a manner to prevent mixups and provide proper identification.

(f) Procedures shall be written describing in sufficient detail the control procedures employed for the issuance of labeling; such written procedures shall be followed.

[43 FR 45077, Sept. 29, 1978, as amended at 58 FR 41354, Aug. 3, 1993; 81 FR 81697, Nov. 18, 2016]

§ 211.130 Packaging and labeling operations.

There shall be written procedures designed to assure that correct labels, labeling, and packaging materials are used for drug products; such written procedures shall be followed. These procedures shall incorporate the following features:

(a) Prevention of mixups and cross-contamination by physical or spatial separation from operations on other drug products.

(b) Identification and handling of filled drug product containers that are set aside and held in unlabeled condition for future labeling operations to preclude mislabeling of individual containers, lots, or portions of lots. Identification need not be applied to each individual container but shall be sufficient to determine name, strength, quantity of contents, and lot or control number of each container.

(c) Identification of the drug product with a lot or control number that permits determination of the history of the manufacture and control of the batch.

(d) Examination of packaging and labeling materials for suitability and correctness before packaging operations, and documentation of such examination in the batch production record.

(e) Inspection of the packaging and labeling facilities immediately before use to assure that all drug products have been removed from previous operations. Inspection shall also be made to assure that packaging and labeling materials not suitable for subsequent operations have been removed. Results of inspection shall be documented in the batch production records.

[43 FR 45077, Sept. 29, 1978, as amended at 58 FR 41354, Aug. 3, 1993]

§ 211.132 Tamper-evident packaging requirements for over-the-counter (OTC) human drug products.

(a) *General.* The Food and Drug Administration has the authority under the Federal Food, Drug, and Cosmetic Act (the act) to establish a uniform national requirement for tamper-evident packaging of OTC drug products that will improve the security of OTC drug packaging and help assure the safety and effectiveness of OTC drug products. An OTC drug product (except a dermatological, dentifrice, insulin, or lozenge product) for retail sale that is not packaged in a tamper-resistant package or that is not properly labeled under this section is adulterated under section 501 of the act or misbranded under section 502 of the act, or both.

(b) *Requirements for tamper-evident package.*

(1) Each manufacturer and packer who packages an OTC drug product (except a dermatological, dentifrice, insulin, or lozenge product) for retail sale shall package the product in a tamper-evident package, if this product is accessible to the public while held for sale. A tamper-evident package is one having one or more indicators or barriers to entry which, if breached or missing, can reasonably be expected to provide visible evidence to consumers that tampering has occurred. To reduce the likelihood of successful tampering and to increase the likelihood that consumers will discover if a product has been tampered with, the package is required to be distinctive by design or by the use of one or more indicators or barriers to entry that employ an identifying characteristic (e.g., a pattern, name, registered trademark, logo, or picture). For purposes of this section, the term "distinctive by design" means the packaging cannot be duplicated with commonly available materials or through commonly available processes. A tamper-evident package may involve an immediate-container and closure system or secondary-container or carton system or any

combination of systems intended to provide a visual indication of package integrity. The tamper-evident feature shall be designed to and shall remain intact when handled in a reasonable manner during manufacture, distribution, and retail display.

(2) In addition to the tamper-evident packaging feature described in paragraph (b)(1) of this section, any two-piece, hard gelatin capsule covered by this section must be sealed using an acceptable tamper-evident technology.

(c) *Labeling.*

(1) In order to alert consumers to the specific tamper-evident feature(s) used, each retail package of an OTC drug product covered by this section (except ammonia inhalant in crushable glass ampules, containers of compressed medical oxygen, or aerosol products that depend upon the power of a liquefied or compressed gas to expel the contents from the container) is required to bear a statement that:

(i) Identifies all tamper-evident feature(s) and any capsule sealing technologies used to comply with paragraph (b) of this section;

(ii) Is prominently placed on the package; and

(iii) Is so placed that it will be unaffected if the tamper-evident feature of the package is breached or missing.

(2) If the tamper-evident feature chosen to meet the requirements in paragraph (b) of this section uses an identifying characteristic, that characteristic is required to

be referred to in the labeling statement. For example, the labeling statement on a bottle with a shrink band could say "For your protection, this bottle has an imprinted seal around the neck."

(d) ***Request for exemptions from packaging and labeling requirements.*** A manufacturer or packer may request an exemption from the packaging and labeling requirements of this section. A request for an exemption is required to be submitted in the form of a citizen petition under § 10.30 of this chapter and should be clearly identified on the envelope as a "Request for Exemption from the Tamper-Evident Packaging Rule." The petition is required to contain the following:

(1) The name of the drug product or, if the petition seeks an exemption for a drug class, the name of the drug class, and a list of products within that class.

(2) The reasons that the drug product's compliance with the tamper-evident packaging or labeling requirements of this section is unnecessary or cannot be achieved.

(3) A description of alternative steps that are available, or that the petitioner has already taken, to reduce the likelihood that the product or drug class will be the subject of malicious adulteration.

(4) Other information justifying an exemption.

(e) ***OTC drug products subject to approved new drug applications.*** Holders of approved new drug applications for OTC drug products are required under § 314.70 of this chapter to provide the agency with notification of changes in packaging and labeling to comply with the requirements of this section. Changes in packaging and labeling required by this regulation may be made before FDA approval, as provided under § 314.70(c) of this chapter. Manufacturing changes by which capsules are to be sealed require prior FDA approval under § 314.70(b) of this chapter.

(f) *Poison Prevention Packaging Act of 1970.* This section does not affect any requirements for "special packaging" as defined under § 310.3(l) of this chapter and required under the Poison Prevention Packaging Act of 1970.

(Approved by the Office of Management and Budget under OMB control number 0910-0149)

[54 FR 5228, Feb. 2, 1989, as amended at 63 FR 59470, Nov. 4, 1998]

§ 211.134 Drug product inspection.

(a) Packaged and labeled products shall be examined during finishing operations to provide assurance that containers and packages in the lot have the correct label.

(b) A representative sample of units shall be collected at the completion of finishing operations and shall be visually examined for correct labeling.

(c) Results of these examinations shall be recorded in the batch production or control records.

§ 211.137 Expiration dating.

(a) To assure that a drug product meets applicable standards of identity, strength, quality, and purity at the time of use, it shall bear an expiration date determined by appropriate stability testing described in § 211.166.

(b) Expiration dates shall be related to any storage conditions stated on the labeling, as determined by stability studies described in § 211.166.

(c) If the drug product is to be reconstituted at the time of dispensing, its labeling shall bear expiration information for both the reconstituted and unreconstituted drug products.

(d) Expiration dates shall appear on labeling in accordance with the requirements of § 201.17 of this chapter.

(e) Homeopathic drug products shall be exempt from the requirements of this section.

(f) Allergenic extracts that are labeled "No U.S. Standard of Potency" are exempt from the requirements of this section.

(g) New drug products for investigational use are exempt from the requirements of this section, provided that they meet appropriate standards or specifications as demonstrated by stability studies during their use in clinical investigations. Where new drug products for investigational use are to be reconstituted at the time of dispensing, their labeling shall bear expiration information for the reconstituted drug product.

(h) Pending consideration of a proposed exemption, published in the Federal Register of September 29, 1978, the requirements in this section shall not be enforced for human OTC drug products if their labeling does not bear dosage limitations and they are stable for at least 3 years as supported by appropriate stability data.

[43 FR 45077, Sept. 29, 1978, as amended at 46 FR 56412, Nov. 17, 1981; 60 FR 4091, Jan. 20, 1995]

SUBPART H - HOLDING AND DISTRIBUTION

§ 211.142 Warehousing procedures.

Written procedures describing the warehousing of drug products shall be established and followed. They shall include:

(a) Quarantine of drug products before release by the quality control unit.

(b) Storage of drug products under appropriate conditions of temperature, humidity, and light so that the identity, strength, quality, and purity of the drug products are not affected.

§ 211.150 Distribution procedures.

Written procedures shall be established, and followed, describing the distribution of drug products. They shall include:

(a) A procedure whereby the oldest approved stock of a drug product is distributed first. Deviation from this requirement is permitted if such deviation is temporary and appropriate.

(b) A system by which the distribution of each lot of drug product can be readily determined to facilitate its recall if necessary.

SUBPART I - LABORATORY CONTROLS

§ 211.160 General requirements.

(a) The establishment of any specifications, standards, sampling plans, test procedures, or other laboratory control mechanisms required by this subpart, including any change in such specifications, standards, sampling plans, test procedures, or other laboratory control mechanisms, shall be drafted by the appropriate organizational unit and reviewed and approved by the quality control unit. The requirements in this subpart shall be followed and shall be documented at the time of performance. Any deviation from the written specifications, standards, sampling plans, test procedures, or other laboratory control mechanisms shall be recorded and justified.

(b) Laboratory controls shall include the establishment of scientifically sound and appropriate specifications, standards, sampling plans, and test procedures designed to assure that components, drug product containers, closures, in-process materials, labeling, and drug products conform to appropriate standards of identity, strength, quality, and purity. Laboratory controls shall include:

(1) Determination of conformity to applicable written specifications for the acceptance of each lot within each shipment of components, drug product containers, closures, and labeling used in the manufacture, processing, packing, or holding of drug products. The specifications shall include a description of the sampling and testing procedures used. Samples shall be representative and adequately identified. Such procedures shall also require appropriate retesting of any component, drug product container, or closure that is subject to deterioration.

(2) Determination of conformance to written specifications and a description of sampling and testing procedures for in-process materials. Such samples shall be representative and properly identified.

(3) Determination of conformance to written descriptions of sampling procedures and appropriate specifications for drug products. Such samples shall be representative and properly identified.

(4) The calibration of instruments, apparatus, gauges, and recording devices at suitable intervals in accordance with an established written program containing specific directions, schedules, limits for accuracy and precision, and provisions for remedial action in the event accuracy and/or precision limits are not met. Instruments, apparatus, gauges, and recording devices not meeting established specifications shall not be used.

[43 FR 45077, Sept. 29, 1978, as amended at 73 FR 51932, Sept. 8, 2008]

§ 211.165 Testing and release for distribution.

(a) For each batch of drug product, there shall be appropriate laboratory determination of satisfactory conformance to final specifications for the drug product, including the identity and strength of each active ingredient, prior to release. Where sterility and/or pyrogen testing are conducted on specific batches of shortlived radiopharmaceuticals, such batches may be released prior to completion of sterility and/or pyrogen testing, provided such testing is completed as soon as possible.

(b) There shall be appropriate laboratory testing, as necessary, of each batch of drug product required to be free of objectionable microorganisms.

(c) Any sampling and testing plans shall be described in written procedures that shall include the method of sampling and the number of units per batch to be tested; such written procedure shall be followed.

(d) Acceptance criteria for the sampling and testing conducted by the quality control unit shall be adequate to assure that batches of drug products meet each appropriate specification and appropriate statistical quality control criteria as a condition for their approval and release. The statistical quality control criteria shall include appropriate acceptance levels and/or appropriate rejection levels.

(e) The accuracy, sensitivity, specificity, and reproducibility of test methods employed by the firm shall be established and documented. Such validation and documentation may be accomplished in accordance with § 211.194(a)(2).

(f) Drug products failing to meet established standards or specifications and any other relevant quality control criteria shall be rejected. Reprocessing may be performed. Prior to acceptance and use, reprocessed material must meet appropriate standards, specifications, and any other relevant criteria.

§ 211.166 Stability testing.

(a) There shall be a written testing program designed to assess the stability characteristics of drug products. The results of such stability testing shall be used in determining appropriate storage conditions and expiration dates. The written program shall be followed and shall include:

(1) Sample size and test intervals based on statistical criteria for each attribute examined to assure valid estimates of stability;

(2) Storage conditions for samples retained for testing;

(3) Reliable, meaningful, and specific test methods;

(4) Testing of the drug product in the same container-closure system as that in which the drug product is marketed;

(5) Testing of drug products for reconstitution at the time of dispensing (as directed in the labeling) as well as after they are reconstituted.

(b) An adequate number of batches of each drug product shall be tested to determine an appropriate expiration date and a record of such data shall be maintained. Accelerated studies, combined with basic stability information on the components, drug products, and container-closure system, may be used to support tentative expiration dates provided full shelf life studies are not available and are being conducted. Where data from accelerated studies are used to project a tentative expiration date that is beyond a date supported by actual shelf life studies, there must be stability studies conducted, including drug product testing at appropriate intervals, until the tentative expiration date is verified or the appropriate expiration date determined.

(c) For homeopathic drug products, the requirements of this section are as follows:

(1) There shall be a written assessment of stability based at least on testing or examination of the drug product for compatibility of the ingredients, and based on marketing experience with the drug product to indicate that there is no degradation of the product for the normal or expected period of use.

(2) Evaluation of stability shall be based on the same container-closure system in which the drug product is being marketed.

(d) Allergenic extracts that are labeled "No U.S. Standard of Potency" are exempt from the requirements of this section.

[43 FR 45077, Sept. 29, 1978, as amended at 46 FR 56412, Nov. 17, 1981]

§ 211.167 Special testing requirements.

(a) For each batch of drug product purporting to be sterile and/or pyrogen-free, there shall be appropriate laboratory testing to determine conformance to such requirements. The test procedures shall be in writing and shall be followed.

(b) For each batch of ophthalmic ointment, there shall be appropriate testing to determine conformance to specifications regarding the presence of foreign particles and harsh or abrasive substances. The test procedures shall be in writing and shall be followed.

(c) For each batch of controlled-release dosage form, there shall be appropriate laboratory testing to determine conformance to the specifications for the rate of release of each active ingredient. The test procedures shall be in writing and shall be followed.

§ 211.170 Reserve samples.

(a) An appropriately identified reserve sample that is representative of each lot in each shipment of each active ingredient shall be retained. The reserve sample consists of at least twice the quantity necessary for all tests required to determine whether the active ingredient meets its established specifications, except for sterility and pyrogen testing. The retention time is as follows:

(1) For an active ingredient in a drug product other than those described in paragraphs (a) (2) and (3) of this section, the reserve sample shall be retained for 1 year after the expiration date of the last lot of the drug product containing the active ingredient.

(2) For an active ingredient in a radioactive drug product, except for nonradioactive reagent kits, the reserve sample shall be retained for:

(i) Three months after the expiration date of the last lot of the drug product containing the active ingredient if the expiration dating period of the drug product is 30 days or less; or

(ii) Six months after the expiration date of the last lot of the drug product containing the active ingredient if the expiration dating period of the drug product is more than 30 days.

(3) For an active ingredient in an OTC drug product that is exempt from bearing an expiration date under § 211.137, the reserve sample shall be retained for 3 years after distribution of the last lot of the drug product containing the active ingredient.

(b) An appropriately identified reserve sample that is representative of each lot or batch of drug product shall be retained and stored under conditions consistent with product labeling. The reserve sample shall be stored in the same immediate container-closure system in which the drug product is marketed or in one that has essentially the same characteristics. The reserve sample consists of at least twice the quantity necessary to perform all the required tests, except those for sterility and pyrogens. Except for those for drug products described in paragraph (b)(2) of this section, reserve samples from representative sample lots or batches selected by acceptable statistical procedures shall be examined visually at least once a year for evidence of deterioration unless visual examination would affect the integrity of the reserve sample. Any evidence of reserve sample deterioration shall be investigated in accordance with § 211.192. The results of the examination shall be recorded and maintained with other stability data on the drug product. Reserve samples of compressed medical gases need not be retained. The retention time is as follows:

(1) For a drug product other than those described in paragraphs (b) (2) and (3) of this section, the reserve sample shall be retained for 1 year after the expiration date of the drug product.

(2) For a radioactive drug product, except for nonradioactive reagent kits, the reserve sample shall be retained for:

(i) Three months after the expiration date of the drug product if the expiration dating period of the drug product is 30 days or less; or

(ii) Six months after the expiration date of the drug product if the expiration dating period of the drug product is more than 30 days.

(3) For an OTC drug product that is exempt for bearing an expiration date under § 211.137, the reserve sample must be retained for 3 years after the lot or batch of drug product is distributed.

[48 FR 13025, Mar. 29, 1983, as amended at 60 FR 4091, Jan. 20, 1995]

§ 211.173 Laboratory animals.

Animals used in testing components, in-process materials, or drug products for compliance with established specifications shall be maintained and controlled in a manner that assures their suitability for their intended use. They shall be identified, and adequate records shall be maintained showing the history of their use.

§ 211.176 Penicillin contamination.

If a reasonable possibility exists that a non-penicillin drug product has been exposed to cross-contamination with penicillin, the non-penicillin drug product shall be tested for the presence of penicillin. Such drug product shall not be marketed if detectable levels are found when tested according to procedures specified in 'Procedures for Detecting and Measuring Penicillin Contamination in Drugs,' which is incorporated by reference. Copies are available from the Division of Research and Testing (HFD-470), Center for Drug Evaluation and Research, Food and Drug Administration, 5001 Campus Dr., College Park, MD 20740, or available for inspection at the National Archives and Records Administration (NARA). For information on the availability of this material at

NARA, call 202-741-6030, or go to: *http://www.archives.gov/federal_register/code_of_federal_regulations/ibr_locations.html*.

[43 FR 45077, Sept. 29, 1978, as amended at 47 FR 9396, Mar. 5, 1982; 50 FR 8996, Mar. 6, 1985; 55 FR 11577, Mar. 29, 1990; 66 FR 56035, Nov. 6, 2001; 69 FR 18803, Apr. 9, 2004; 81 FR 49897, July 29, 2016]

SUBPART J - RECORDS AND REPORTS

§ 211.180 General requirements.

(a) Any production, control, or distribution record that is required to be maintained in compliance with this part and is specifically associated with a batch of a drug product shall be retained for at least 1 year after the expiration date of the batch or, in the case of certain OTC drug products lacking expiration dating because they meet the criteria for exemption under § 211.137, 3 years after distribution of the batch.

(b) Records shall be maintained for all components, drug product containers, closures, and labeling for at least 1 year after the expiration date or, in the case of certain OTC drug products lacking expiration dating because they meet the criteria for exemption under § 211.137, 3 years after distribution of the last lot of drug product incorporating the component or using the container, closure, or labeling.

(c) All records required under this part, or copies of such records, shall be readily available for authorized inspection during the retention period at the establishment where the activities described in such records occurred.

These records or copies thereof shall be subject to photocopying or other means of reproduction as part of such inspection. Records that can be immediately retrieved from another location by computer or other electronic means shall be considered as meeting the requirements of this paragraph.

(d) Records required under this part may be retained either as original records or as true copies such as photocopies, microfilm, microfiche, or other accurate reproductions of the original records. Where reduction techniques, such as microfilming, are used, suitable reader and photocopying equipment shall be readily available.

(e) Written records required by this part shall be maintained so that data therein can be used for evaluating, at least annually, the quality standards of each drug product to determine the need for changes in drug product specifications or manufacturing or control procedures. Written procedures shall be established and followed for such evaluations and shall include provisions for:

(1) A review of a representative number of batches, whether approved or rejected, and, where applicable, records associated with the batch.

(2) A review of complaints, recalls, returned or salvaged drug products, and investigations conducted under § 211.192 for each drug product.

(f) Procedures shall be established to assure that the responsible officials of the firm, if they are not personally involved in or immediately aware of such actions, are notified in writing of any investigations conducted under §§ 211.198, 211.204, or 211.208 of these regulations, any recalls, reports of inspectional observations issued by the Food and Drug Administration, or any regulatory actions relating to good manufacturing practices brought by the Food and Drug Administration.

[43 FR 45077, Sept. 29, 1978, as amended at 60 FR 4091, Jan. 20, 1995]

§ 211.182 Equipment cleaning and use log.

A written record of major equipment cleaning, maintenance (except routine maintenance such as lubrication and adjustments), and use shall be included in individual equipment logs that show the date, time, product, and lot number of each batch processed. If equipment is dedicated to manufacture of one product, then individual equipment logs are not required, provided that lots or batches of such product follow in numerical order and are manufactured in numerical sequence. In cases where dedicated equipment is employed, the records of cleaning, maintenance, and use shall be part of the batch record. The persons performing and double-checking the cleaning and maintenance (or, if the cleaning and maintenance is performed using automated equipment under § 211.68, just the person verifying the cleaning and maintenance done by the automated equipment) shall date and sign or initial the log indicating that the work was performed. Entries in the log shall be in chronological order.

[73 FR 51933, Sept. 8, 2008]

§ 211.184 Component, drug product container, closure, and labeling records.

These records shall include the following:

(a) The identity and quantity of each shipment of each lot of components, drug product containers, closures, and labeling; the name of the supplier; the supplier's lot number(s) if known; the receiving code as specified in § 211.80; and the date of receipt. The name and location of the prime manufacturer, if different from the supplier, shall be listed if known.

(b) The results of any test or examination performed (including those performed as required by § 211.82(a), § 211.84(d), or § 211.122(a)) and the conclusions derived therefrom.

(c) An individual inventory record of each component, drug product container, and closure and, for each component, a reconciliation of the use of each lot of such component. The inventory record shall contain sufficient information to allow determination of any batch or lot of drug product associated with the use of each component, drug product container, and closure.

(d) Documentation of the examination and review of labels and labeling for conformity with established specifications in accord with §§ 211.122(c) and 211.130(c).

(e) The disposition of rejected components, drug product containers, closure, and labeling.

§ 211.186 Master production and control records.

(a) To assure uniformity from batch to batch, master production and control records for each drug product, including each batch size thereof, shall be prepared, dated, and signed (full signature, handwritten) by one person and independently checked, dated, and signed by a second person. The preparation of master production and control records shall be described in a written procedure and such written procedure shall be followed.

(b) Master production and control records shall include:

(1) The name and strength of the product and a description of the dosage form;

(2) The name and weight or measure of each active ingredient per dosage unit or per unit of weight or measure of the drug product, and a statement of the total weight or measure of any dosage unit;

(3) A complete list of components designated by names or codes sufficiently specific to indicate any special quality characteristic;

(4) An accurate statement of the weight or measure of each component, using the same weight system (metric, avoirdupois, or apothecary) for each component. Reasonable variations may be permitted, however, in the amount of components necessary for the preparation in the dosage form, provided they are justified in the master production and control records;

(5) A statement concerning any calculated excess of component;

(6) A statement of theoretical weight or measure at appropriate phases of processing;

(7) A statement of theoretical yield, including the maximum and minimum percentages of theoretical yield beyond which investigation according to § 211.192 is required;

(8) A description of the drug product containers, closures, and packaging materials, including a specimen or copy of each label and all other labeling signed and dated by the person or persons responsible for approval of such labeling;

(9) Complete manufacturing and control instructions, sampling and testing procedures, specifications, special notations, and precautions to be followed.

§ 211.188 Batch production and control records.

Batch production and control records shall be prepared for each batch of drug product produced and shall include complete information relating to the production and control of each batch. These records shall include:

(a) An accurate reproduction of the appropriate master production or control record, checked for accuracy, dated, and signed;

(b) Documentation that each significant step in the manufacture, processing, packing, or holding of the batch was accomplished, including:

(1) Dates;

(2) Identity of individual major equipment and lines used;

(3) Specific identification of each batch of component or in-process material used;

(4) Weights and measures of components used in the course of processing;

(5) In-process and laboratory control results;

(6) Inspection of the packaging and labeling area before and after use;

(7) A statement of the actual yield and a statement of the percentage of theoretical yield at appropriate phases of processing;

(8) Complete labeling control records, including specimens or copies of all labeling used;

(9) Description of drug product containers and closures;

(10) Any sampling performed;

(11) Identification of the persons performing and directly supervising or checking each significant step in the operation, or if a significant step in the operation is performed by automated equipment under § 211.68, the

identification of the person checking the significant step performed by the automated equipment.

(12) Any investigation made according to § 211.192.

(13) Results of examinations made in accordance with § 211.134.

[43 FR 45077, Sept. 29, 1978, as amended at 73 FR 51933, Sept. 8, 2008]

§ 211.192 Production record review.

All drug product production and control records, including those for packaging and labeling, shall be reviewed and approved by the quality control unit to determine compliance with all established, approved written procedures before a batch is released or distributed. Any unexplained discrepancy (including a percentage of theoretical yield exceeding the maximum or minimum percentages established in master production and control records) or the failure of a batch or any of its components to meet any of its specifications shall be thoroughly investigated, whether or not the batch has already been distributed. The investigation shall extend to other batches of the same drug product and other drug products that may have been associated with the specific failure or discrepancy. A written record of the investigation shall be made and shall include the conclusions and followup.

§ 211.194 Laboratory records.

(a) Laboratory records shall include complete data derived from all tests necessary to assure compliance with established specifications and standards, including examinations and assays, as follows:

(1) A description of the sample received for testing with identification of source (that is, location from where sample was obtained), quantity, lot number or other distinctive code, date sample was taken, and date sample was received for testing.

(2) A statement of each method used in the testing of the sample. The statement shall indicate the location of data that establish that the methods used in the testing of the sample meet proper standards of accuracy and reliability as applied to the product tested. (If the method employed is in the current revision of the United States Pharmacopeia, National Formulary, AOAC INTERNATIONAL, Book of Methods,[1] or in other recognized standard references, or is detailed in an approved new drug application and the referenced method is not modified, a statement indicating the method and reference will suffice). The suitability of all testing methods used shall be verified under actual conditions of use.

(3) A statement of the weight or measure of sample used for each test, where appropriate.

(4) A complete record of all data secured in the course of each test, including all graphs, charts, and spectra from laboratory instrumentation, properly identified to show the specific component, drug product container, closure, in-process material, or drug product, and lot tested.

(5) A record of all calculations performed in connection with the test, including units of measure, conversion factors, and equivalency factors.

(6) A statement of the results of tests and how the results compare with established standards of identity, strength, quality, and purity for the component, drug product container, closure, in-process material, or drug product tested.

(7) The initials or signature of the person who performs each test and the date(s) the tests were performed.

(8) The initials or signature of a second person showing that the original records have been reviewed for accuracy, completeness, and compliance with established standards.

(b) Complete records shall be maintained of any modification of an established method employed in testing. Such records shall include the reason for the modification and data to verify that the modification produced results that are at least as accurate and reliable for the material being tested as the established method.

(c) Complete records shall be maintained of any testing and standardization of laboratory reference standards, reagents, and standard solutions.

(d) Complete records shall be maintained of the periodic calibration of laboratory instruments, apparatus, gauges, and recording devices required by § 211.160(b)(4).

(e) Complete records shall be maintained of all stability testing performed in accordance with § 211.166.

[43 FR 45077, Sept. 29, 1978, as amended at 55 FR 11577, Mar. 29, 1990; 65 FR 18889, Apr. 10, 2000; 70 FR 40880, July 15, 2005; 70 FR 67651, Nov. 8, 2005]

Footnotes - 211.194

[1] Copies may be obtained from: AOAC INTERNATIONAL, 481 North Frederick Ave., suite 500, Gaithersburg, MD 20877.

§ 211.196 Distribution records.

Distribution records shall contain the name and strength of the product and description of the dosage form, name and address of the consignee, date and quantity shipped, and lot or control number of the drug product. For compressed medical gas products, distribution records are not required to contain lot or control numbers.

(Approved by the Office of Management and Budget under control number 0910-0139)

[49 FR 9865, Mar. 16, 1984]

§ 211.198 Complaint files.

(a) Written procedures describing the handling of all written and oral complaints regarding a drug product shall be established and followed. Such procedures shall include provisions for review by the quality control unit, of any complaint involving the possible failure of a drug product to meet any of its specifications and, for such drug products, a determination as to the need for an investigation in accordance with § 211.192. Such procedures shall include provisions for review to determine whether the complaint represents a serious and unexpected adverse drug experience which is required to be reported to the Food and Drug Administration in accordance with §§ 310.305 and 514.80 of this chapter.

(b) A written record of each complaint shall be maintained in a file designated for drug product complaints. The file regarding such drug product complaints shall be maintained at the establishment where the drug product involved was manufactured, processed, or packed, or such file may be maintained at another facility if the written records in such files are readily available for inspection at that other facility. Written records involving a drug product shall be maintained until at least 1 year after the expiration date of the drug product, or 1 year after the date that the complaint was received, whichever is longer. In the case of certain OTC drug products lacking expiration dating because they meet the criteria for exemption under § 211.137, such written records shall be maintained for 3 years after distribution of the drug product.

(1) The written record shall include the following information, where known: the name and strength of the drug product, lot number, name of complainant, nature of complaint, and reply to complainant.

(2) Where an investigation under § 211.192 is conducted, the written record shall include the findings of the investigation and followup. The record or copy of the record of the investigation shall be maintained at the establishment where the investigation occurred in accordance with § 211.180(c).

(3) Where an investigation under § 211.192 is not conducted, the written record shall include the reason that an investigation was found not to be necessary and the name of the responsible person making such a determination.

[43 FR 45077, Sept. 29, 1978, as amended at 51 FR 24479, July 3, 1986; 68 FR 15364, Mar. 31, 2003]

SUBPART K - RETURNED AND SALVAGED DRUG PRODUCTS

§ 211.204 Returned drug products.

Returned drug products shall be identified as such and held. If the conditions under which returned drug products have been held, stored, or shipped before or during their return, or if the condition of the drug product, its container, carton, or labeling, as a result of storage or shipping, casts doubt on the safety, identity, strength, quality or purity of the drug product, the returned drug product shall be destroyed unless examination, testing, or other investigations prove the drug product meets appropriate standards of safety, identity, strength, quality, or purity. A drug product may be reprocessed provided the subsequent drug product meets appropriate standards, specifications, and characteristics. Records of returned drug products shall be maintained and shall include the name and label potency of the drug product dosage form, lot number (or control number or batch number), reason for the return, quantity returned, date of disposition, and ultimate disposition of the returned drug product. If the reason for a drug product being returned implicates associated batches, an appropriate investigation shall be conducted in accordance with the requirements of § 211.192. Procedures for the holding, testing, and reprocessing of returned drug products shall be in writing and shall be followed.

§ 211.208 Drug product salvaging.

Drug products that have been subjected to improper storage conditions including extremes in temperature, humidity, smoke, fumes, pressure, age, or radiation due to natural disasters, fires, accidents, or equipment failures shall not be salvaged and returned to the marketplace. Whenever there is a question whether drug products have been subjected to such conditions, salvaging operations may be conducted only if there is (a) evidence from laboratory tests and assays (including animal feeding studies where applicable) that the drug products meet all applicable standards of identity, strength, quality, and purity and (b) evidence from inspection of the premises that the drug products and their associated packaging were not subjected to improper storage conditions as a result of the disaster or accident. Organoleptic examinations shall be acceptable only as supplemental evidence that the drug products meet appropriate standards of identity, strength, quality, and purity. Records including name, lot number, and disposition shall be maintained for drug products subject to this section.

Title 21
Food and Drugs

Chapter I
Food and Drug Administration, Department of Health and Human Services

Subchapter H – Medical Devices

Part 820
Quality System Regulation

Subpart A - General Provisions
§ 820.1 Scope.
§ 820.3 Definitions.
§ 820.5 Quality system.
Subpart B - Quality System Requirements
§ 820.20 Management responsibility.
§ 820.22 Quality audit.
§ 820.25 Personnel.
Subpart C – Design Controls
§ 820.30 Design controls.
Subpart D – Document Controls
§ 820.40 Document controls.
Subpart E – Purchasing Controls
§ 820.50 Purchasing controls.
Subpart F – Identification and Traceability
§ 820.60 Identification.

§ 820.65 Traceability.

Subpart G – Production and Process Controls

§ 820.70 Production and process controls.

§ 820.72 Inspection, measuring, and test equipment.

§ 820.75 Process validation.

Subpart H – Acceptance Activities

§ 820.80 Receiving, in-process, and finished device acceptance.

§ 820.86 Acceptance status.

Subpart I – Nonconforming Product

§ 820.90 Nonconforming product.

Subpart J – Corrective and Preventive Action

§ 820.100 Corrective and preventive action.

Subpart K – Labeling and packaging Control

§ 820.120 Device labeling.

§ 820.130 Device packaging.

Subpart L – Handling, Storage, Distribution, and Installation

§ 820.140 Handling.

§ 820.150 Storage.

§ 820.160 Distribution.

§ 820.170 Installation.

Subpart M – Records

§ 820.180 General requirements.

§ 820.181 Device master record.

§ 820.184 Device history record.

§ 820.186 Quality system record.

§ 820.198 Complaint files.

Subpart N – Servicing

§ 820.200 Servicing.

Subpart O – Statistical Techniques

§ 820.250 Statistical techniques.

Authority: 21 U.S.C. 351, 352, 360, 360c, 360d, 360e, 360h, 360i, 360j, 360l, 371, 374, 381, 383; 42 U.S.C. 216, 262, 263a, 264.

Source: 61 FR 52654, Oct. 7, 1996, unless otherwise noted.

SUBPART A - GENERAL PROVISIONS

§ 820.1 Scope.

(a) *Applicability.*

(1) Current good manufacturing practice (CGMP) requirements are set forth in this quality system regulation. The requirements in this part govern the methods used in, and the facilities and controls used for, the design, manufacture, packaging, labeling, storage, installation, and servicing of all finished devices intended for human use. The requirements in this part are intended to ensure that finished devices will be safe and effective and otherwise in compliance with the Federal Food, Drug, and Cosmetic Act (the act). This part establishes basic requirements applicable to manufacturers of finished medical devices. If a manufacturer engages in only some operations subject to the requirements in this part, and not in others, that manufacturer need only comply with those requirements applicable to the operations in which it is engaged. With respect to class I devices, design controls apply only to those devices listed in § 820.30(a)(2). This regulation does not apply to manufacturers of components or parts of finished devices, but such manufacturers are encouraged to use appropriate provisions of this regulation as guidance. Manufacturers of blood and blood components used for transfusion or for further

manufacturing are not subject to this part, but are subject to subchapter F of this chapter. Manufacturers of human cells, tissues, and cellular and tissue-based products (HCT/Ps), as defined in § 1271.3(d) of this chapter, that are medical devices (subject to premarket review or notification, or exempt from notification, under an application submitted under the device provisions of the act or under a biological product license application under section 351 of the Public Health Service Act) are subject to this part and are also subject to the donor-eligibility procedures set forth in part 1271 subpart C of this chapter and applicable current good tissue practice procedures in part 1271 subpart D of this chapter. In the event of a conflict between applicable regulations in part 1271 and in other parts of this chapter, the regulation specifically applicable to the device in question shall supersede the more general.

(2) The provisions of this part shall be applicable to any finished device as defined in this part, intended for human use, that is manufactured, imported, or offered for import in any State or Territory of the United States, the District of Columbia, or the Commonwealth of Puerto Rico.

(3) In this regulation the term "where appropriate" is used several times. When a requirement is qualified by "where appropriate," it is deemed to be "appropriate" unless the manufacturer can document justification otherwise. A requirement is "appropriate" if nonimplementation could reasonably be expected to result in the product not meeting its specified requirements or the manufacturer not being able to carry out any necessary corrective action.

(b) The quality system regulation in this part supplements regulations in other parts of this chapter except where explicitly stated otherwise. In the event of a conflict between applicable regulations in this part and in other parts of this chapter, the regulations specifically applicable to the device in question shall supersede any other generally applicable requirements.

(c) *Authority.* Part 820 is established and issued under authority of sections 501, 502, 510, 513, 514, 515, 518, 519, 520, 522, 701, 704, 801, 803 of the act (21 U.S.C. 351, 352, 360, 360c, 360d, 360e, 360h, 360i, 360j, 360l, 371, 374, 381, 383). The failure to comply with any applicable provision in this part renders a device adulterated under section 501(h) of the act. Such a device, as well as any person responsible for the failure to comply, is subject to regulatory action.

(d) *Foreign manufacturers.* If a manufacturer who offers devices for import into the United States refuses to permit or allow the completion of a Food and Drug Administration (FDA) inspection of the foreign facility for the purpose of determining compliance with this part, it shall appear for purposes of section 801(a) of the act, that the methods used in, and the facilities and controls used for, the design, manufacture, packaging, labeling, storage, installation, or servicing of any devices produced at such facility that are offered for import into the United States do not conform to the requirements of section 520(f) of the act and this part and that the devices manufactured at that facility are adulterated under section 501(h) of the act.

(e) *Exemptions or variances.*

(1) Any person who wishes to petition for an exemption or variance from any device quality system requirement is subject to the requirements of section 520(f)(2) of the Federal Food, Drug, and Cosmetic Act. Petitions for an exemption or variance shall be submitted according to the procedures set forth in § 10.30 of this chapter, the FDA's administrative procedures. For guidance on how to proceed for a request for a variance, contact Division of Regulatory Programs 2, Office of Regulatory Programs, Office of Product Evaluation and Quality, Center for Devices and Radiological Health, Food and Drug Administration, 10903 New Hampshire Ave., Bldg. 66, Rm. 1438, Silver Spring, MD 20993-0002.

(2) FDA may initiate and grant a variance from any device quality system requirement when the agency determines that such variance is in the best interest of the public health. Such variance will remain in effect only so long as there remains a public health need for the device and the device would not likely be made sufficiently available without the variance.

[61 FR 52654, Oct. 7, 1996, as amended at 65 FR 17136, Mar. 31, 2000; 65 FR 66636, Nov. 7, 2000; 69 FR 29829, May 25, 2005; 72 FR 17399, Apr. 9, 2007; 75 FR 20915, Apr. 22, 2010; 80 FR 29906, May 22, 2015; 85 FR 18442, Apr. 2, 2020]

§ 820.3 Definitions.

(a) *Act* means the Federal Food, Drug, and Cosmetic Act, as amended (secs. 201-903, 52 Stat. 1040 *et seq.,* as amended (21 U.S.C. 321-394)). All definitions in section 201 of the act shall apply to the regulations in this part.

(b) *Complaint* means any written, electronic, or oral communication that alleges deficiencies related to the identity, quality, durability, reliability, safety, effectiveness, or performance of a device after it is released for distribution.

(c) *Component* means any raw material, substance, piece, part, software, firmware, labeling, or assembly which is intended to be included as part of the finished, packaged, and labeled device.

(d) *Control number* means any distinctive symbols, such as a distinctive combination of letters or numbers, or both, from which the history of the manufacturing, packaging, labeling, and distribution of a unit, lot, or batch of finished devices can be determined.

(e) *Design history file* (*DHF*) means a compilation of records which describes the design history of a finished device.

(f) *Design input* means the physical and performance requirements of a device that are used as a basis for device design.

(g) *Design output* means the results of a design effort at each design phase and at the end of the total design effort. The finished design output is the basis for the device master record. The total finished design output consists of the device, its packaging and labeling, and the device master record.

(h) *Design review* means a documented, comprehensive, systematic examination of a design to evaluate the adequacy of the design requirements, to evaluate the capability of the design to meet these requirements, and to identify problems.

(i) *Device history record* (*DHR*) means a compilation of records containing the production history of a finished device.

(j) *Device master record* (*DMR*) means a compilation of records containing the procedures and specifications for a finished device.

(k) *Establish* means define, document (in writing or electronically), and implement.

(l) *Finished device* means any device or accessory to any device that is suitable for use or capable of functioning, whether or not it is packaged, labeled, or sterilized.

(m) *Lot or batch* means one or more components or finished devices that consist of a single type, model, class, size, composition, or software version that are manufactured under essentially the same conditions and that are intended to have uniform characteristics and quality within specified limits.

(n) *Management with executive responsibility* means those senior employees of a manufacturer who have the authority to establish or make changes to the manufacturer's quality policy and quality system.

(o) ***Manufacturer*** means any person who designs, manufactures, fabricates, assembles, or processes a finished device. Manufacturer includes but is not limited to those who perform the functions of contract sterilization, installation, relabeling, remanufacturing, repacking, or specification development, and initial distributors of foreign entities performing these functions.

(p) ***Manufacturing material*** means any material or substance used in or used to facilitate the manufacturing process, a concomitant constituent, or a byproduct constituent produced during the manufacturing process, which is present in or on the finished device as a residue or impurity not by design or intent of the manufacturer.

(q) ***Nonconformity*** means the nonfulfillment of a specified requirement.

(r) ***Product*** means components, manufacturing materials, in- process devices, finished devices, and returned devices.

(s) ***Quality*** means the totality of features and characteristics that bear on the ability of a device to satisfy fitness-for-use, including safety and performance.

(t) ***Quality audit*** means a systematic, independent examination of a manufacturer's quality system that is performed at defined intervals and at sufficient frequency to determine whether both quality system activities and the results of such activities comply with quality system procedures, that these procedures are implemented effectively, and that these procedures are suitable to achieve quality system objectives.

(u) *Quality policy* means the overall intentions and direction of an organization with respect to quality, as established by management with executive responsibility.

(v) *Quality system* means the organizational structure, responsibilities, procedures, processes, and resources for implementing quality management.

(w) *Remanufacturer* means any person who processes, conditions, renovates, repackages, restores, or does any other act to a finished device that significantly changes the finished device's performance or safety specifications, or intended use.

(x) *Rework* means action taken on a nonconforming product so that it will fulfill the specified DMR requirements before it is released for distribution.

(y) *Specification* means any requirement with which a product, process, service, or other activity must conform.

(z) *Validation* means confirmation by examination and provision of objective evidence that the particular requirements for a specific intended use can be consistently fulfilled.

(1) *Process validation* means establishing by objective evidence that a process consistently produces a result or product meeting its predetermined specifications.

(2) *Design validation* means establishing by objective evidence that device specifications conform with user needs and intended use(s).

(aa) *Verification* means confirmation by examination and provision of objective evidence that specified requirements have been fulfilled.

(bb) *Human cell, tissue, or cellular or tissue-based product (HCT/P) regulated as a device* means an HCT/P as defined in § 1271.3(d) of this chapter that does not meet the criteria in § 1271.10(a) and that is also regulated as a device.

(cc) *Unique device identifier (UDI)* means an identifier that adequately identifies a device through its distribution and use by meeting the requirements of § 830.20 of this chapter. A unique device identifier is composed of:

(1) A *device identifier* - a mandatory, fixed portion of a UDI that identifies the specific version or model of a device and the labeler of that device; and

(2) A *production identifier* - a conditional, variable portion of a UDI that identifies one or more of the following when included on the label of the device:

(i) The lot or batch within which a device was manufactured;

(ii) The serial number of a specific device;

(iii) The expiration date of a specific device;

(iv) The date a specific device was manufactured.

(v) For an HCT/P regulated as a device, the distinct identification code required by § 1271.290(c) of this chapter.

(dd) *Universal product code (UPC)* means the product identifier used to identify an item sold at retail in the United States.

[61 FR 52654, Oct. 7, 1996, as amended at 78 FR 58822, Sept. 24, 2013]

§ 820.5 Quality system.

Each manufacturer shall establish and maintain a quality system that is appropriate for the specific medical device(s) designed or manufactured, and that meets the requirements of this part.

SUBPART B - QUALITY SYSTEM REQUIREMENTS

§ 820.20 Management responsibility.

(a) *Quality policy.* Management with executive responsibility shall establish its policy and objectives for, and commitment to, quality. Management with executive responsibility shall ensure that the quality policy is understood, implemented, and maintained at all levels of the organization.

(b) *Organization.* Each manufacturer shall establish and maintain an adequate organizational structure to ensure that devices are designed and produced in accordance with the requirements of this part.

(1) *Responsibility and authority.* Each manufacturer shall establish the appropriate responsibility, authority, and interrelation of all personnel who manage, perform, and assess work affecting quality, and provide the independence and authority necessary to perform these tasks.

(2) *Resources.* Each manufacturer shall provide adequate resources, including the assignment of trained personnel, for management, performance of work, and assessment activities, including internal quality audits, to meet the requirements of this part.

(3) *Management representative.* Management with executive responsibility shall appoint, and document such appointment of, a member of management who, irrespective of other responsibilities, shall have established authority over and responsibility for:

(i) Ensuring that quality system requirements are effectively established and effectively maintained in accordance with this part; and

(ii) Reporting on the performance of the quality system to management with executive responsibility for review.

(c) *Management review.* Management with executive responsibility shall review the suitability and effectiveness of the quality system at defined intervals and with sufficient frequency according to established procedures to ensure that the quality system satisfies the requirements of this part and the manufacturer's established quality policy and objectives. The dates and results of quality system reviews shall be documented.

(d) *Quality planning.* Each manufacturer shall establish a quality plan which defines the quality practices, resources, and activities relevant to devices that are designed and manufactured. The manufacturer shall establish how the requirements for quality will be met.

(e) *Quality system procedures.* Each manufacturer shall establish quality system procedures and instructions. An outline of the structure of the documentation used in the quality system shall be established where appropriate.

§ 820.22 Quality audit.

Each manufacturer shall establish procedures for quality audits and conduct such audits to assure that the quality system is in compliance with the established quality system requirements and to determine the effectiveness of the quality system. Quality audits shall be conducted by individuals who do not have direct responsibility for the matters being audited. Corrective action(s), including a reaudit of deficient matters, shall be taken when necessary. A report of the results of each quality audit, and reaudit(s) where taken, shall be made and such reports shall be reviewed by management having responsibility for the matters audited. The dates and results of quality audits and reaudits shall be documented.

§ 820.25 Personnel.

(a) ***General.*** Each manufacturer shall have sufficient personnel with the necessary education, background, training, and experience to assure that all activities required by this part are correctly performed.

(b) ***Training.*** Each manufacturer shall establish procedures for identifying training needs and ensure that all personnel are trained to adequately perform their assigned responsibilities. Training shall be documented.

(1) As part of their training, personnel shall be made aware of device defects which may occur from the improper performance of their specific jobs.

(2) Personnel who perform verification and validation activities shall be made aware of defects and errors that may be encountered as part of their job functions.

SUBPART C - DESIGN CONTROLS

§ 820.30 Design controls.

(a) ***General.***

(1) Each manufacturer of any class III or class II device, and the class I devices listed in paragraph (a)(2) of this section, shall establish and maintain procedures to control the design of the device in order to ensure that specified design requirements are met.

(2) The following class I devices are subject to design controls:

(i) Devices automated with computer software; and

(ii) The devices listed in the following chart.

Section	Device

868.6810 Catheter, Tracheobronchial Suction.

878.4460 Glove, Surgeon's.

880.6760 Restraint, Protective.

892.5650 System, Applicator, Radionuclide, Manual.

892.5740 Source, Radionuclide Teletherapy.

(b) *Design and development planning.* Each manufacturer shall establish and maintain plans that describe or reference the design and development activities and define responsibility for implementation. The plans shall identify and describe the interfaces with different groups or activities that provide, or result in, input to the design and development process. The plans shall be reviewed, updated, and approved as design and development evolves.

(c) *Design input.* Each manufacturer shall establish and maintain procedures to ensure that the design requirements relating to a device are appropriate and address the intended use of the device, including the needs of the user and patient. The procedures shall include a mechanism for addressing incomplete, ambiguous, or conflicting requirements. The design input requirements shall be documented and shall be reviewed and approved by a designated individual(s). The approval, including the date and signature of the individual(s) approving the requirements, shall be documented.

(d) *Design output.* Each manufacturer shall establish and maintain procedures for defining and documenting design output in terms that allow an adequate evaluation of conformance to design input requirements. Design output procedures shall contain or make reference to acceptance criteria and shall ensure that those design outputs that are essential for the proper functioning of the device are identified. Design output shall be documented, reviewed, and approved before release. The approval, including the date and signature of the individual(s) approving the output, shall be documented.

(e) *Design review.* Each manufacturer shall establish and maintain procedures to ensure that formal documented reviews of the design results are planned and conducted at appropriate stages of the device's design development. The procedures shall ensure that participants at each design review include representatives of all functions concerned with the design stage being reviewed and an individual(s) who does not have direct responsibility for the design stage being reviewed, as well as any specialists needed. The results of a design review, including identification of the design, the date, and the individual(s) performing the review, shall be documented in the design history file (the DHF).

(f) ***Design verification.*** Each manufacturer shall establish and maintain procedures for verifying the device design. Design verification shall confirm that the design output meets the design input requirements. The results of the design verification, including identification of the design, method(s), the date, and the individual(s) performing the verification, shall be documented in the DHF.

(g) ***Design validation.*** Each manufacturer shall establish and maintain procedures for validating the device design. Design validation shall be performed under defined operating conditions on initial production units, lots, or batches, or their equivalents. Design validation shall ensure that devices conform to defined user needs and intended uses and shall include testing of production units under actual or simulated use conditions. Design validation shall include software validation and risk analysis, where appropriate. The results of the design validation, including identification of the design, method(s), the date, and the individual(s) performing the validation, shall be documented in the DHF.

(h) ***Design transfer.*** Each manufacturer shall establish and maintain procedures to ensure that the device design is correctly translated into production specifications.

(i) ***Design changes.*** Each manufacturer shall establish and maintain procedures for the identification, documentation, validation or where appropriate verification, review, and approval of design changes before their implementation.

(j) ***Design history file.*** Each manufacturer shall establish and maintain a DHF for each type of device. The DHF shall contain or reference the records necessary to demonstrate that the design was developed in accordance with the approved design plan and the requirements of this part.

SUBPART D - DOCUMENT CONTROLS

§ 820.40 Document controls.

Each manufacturer shall establish and maintain procedures to control all documents that are required by this part. The procedures shall provide for the following:

(a) *Document approval and distribution.* Each manufacturer shall designate an individual(s) to review for adequacy and approve prior to issuance all documents established to meet the requirements of this part. The approval, including the date and signature of the individual(s) approving the document, shall be documented. Documents established to meet the requirements of this part shall be available at all locations for which they are designated, used, or otherwise necessary, and all obsolete documents shall be promptly removed from all points of use or otherwise prevented from unintended use.

(b) *Document changes.* Changes to documents shall be reviewed and approved by an individual(s) in the same function or organization that performed the original review and approval, unless specifically designated otherwise. Approved changes shall be communicated to the appropriate personnel in a timely manner. Each manufacturer shall maintain records of changes to documents. Change records shall include a description of the change, identification of the affected documents, the signature of the approving individual(s), the approval date, and when the change becomes effective.

SUBPART E - PURCHASING CONTROLS

§ 820.50 Purchasing controls.

Each manufacturer shall establish and maintain procedures to ensure that all purchased or otherwise received product and services conform to specified requirements.

(a) *Evaluation of suppliers, contractors, and consultants.* Each manufacturer shall establish and maintain the requirements, including quality requirements, that must be met by suppliers, contractors, and consultants. Each manufacturer shall:

(1) Evaluate and select potential suppliers, contractors, and consultants on the basis of their ability to meet specified requirements, including quality requirements. The evaluation shall be documented.

(2) Define the type and extent of control to be exercised over the product, services, suppliers, contractors, and consultants, based on the evaluation results.

(3) Establish and maintain records of acceptable suppliers, contractors, and consultants.

(b) *Purchasing data.* Each manufacturer shall establish and maintain data that clearly describe or reference the specified requirements, including quality requirements, for purchased or otherwise received product and services. Purchasing documents shall include, where possible, an agreement that the suppliers, contractors, and consultants agree to notify the manufacturer of changes in the product or service so that manufacturers may determine whether the changes may affect the quality of a finished device. Purchasing data shall be approved in accordance with § 820.40.

SUBPART F - IDENTIFICATION AND TRACEABILITY

§ 820.60 Identification.

Each manufacturer shall establish and maintain procedures for identifying product during all stages of receipt, production, distribution, and installation to prevent mixups.

§ 820.65 Traceability.

Each manufacturer of a device that is intended for surgical implant into the body or to support or sustain life and whose failure to perform when properly used in accordance with instructions for use provided in the labeling can be reasonably expected to result in a significant injury to the user shall establish and maintain procedures for identifying with a control number each unit, lot, or batch of finished devices and where appropriate components. The procedures shall facilitate corrective action. Such identification shall be documented in the DHR.

SUBPART G - PRODUCTION AND PROCESS CONTROLS

§ 820.70 Production and process controls.

(a) *General.* Each manufacturer shall develop, conduct, control, and monitor production processes to ensure that a device conforms to its specifications. Where deviations from device specifications could occur as a result of the manufacturing process, the manufacturer shall establish and maintain process control procedures that describe any process controls necessary to ensure conformance to specifications. Where process controls are needed they shall include:

(1) Documented instructions, standard operating procedures (SOP's), and methods that define and control the manner of production;

(2) Monitoring and control of process parameters and component and device characteristics during production;

(3) Compliance with specified reference standards or codes;

(4) The approval of processes and process equipment; and

(5) Criteria for workmanship which shall be expressed in documented standards or by means of identified and approved representative samples.

(b) *Production and process changes.* Each manufacturer shall establish and maintain procedures for changes to a specification, method, process, or procedure. Such changes shall be verified or where appropriate validated according to § 820.75, before implementation and these activities shall be documented. Changes shall be approved in accordance with § 820.40.

(c) ***Environmental control.*** Where environmental conditions could reasonably be expected to have an adverse effect on product quality, the manufacturer shall establish and maintain procedures to adequately control these environmental conditions. Environmental control system(s) shall be periodically inspected to verify that the system, including necessary equipment, is adequate and functioning properly. These activities shall be documented and reviewed.

(d) ***Personnel.*** Each manufacturer shall establish and maintain requirements for the health, cleanliness, personal practices, and clothing of personnel if contact between such personnel and product or environment could reasonably be expected to have an adverse effect on product quality. The manufacturer shall ensure that maintenance and other personnel who are required to work temporarily under special environmental conditions are appropriately trained or supervised by a trained individual.

(e) ***Contamination control.*** Each manufacturer shall establish and maintain procedures to prevent contamination of equipment or product by substances that could reasonably be expected to have an adverse effect on product quality.

(f) ***Buildings.*** Buildings shall be of suitable design and contain sufficient space to perform necessary operations, prevent mixups, and assure orderly handling.

(g) *Equipment.* Each manufacturer shall ensure that all equipment used in the manufacturing process meets specified requirements and is appropriately designed, constructed, placed, and installed to facilitate maintenance, adjustment, cleaning, and use.

(1) *Maintenance schedule.* Each manufacturer shall establish and maintain schedules for the adjustment, cleaning, and other maintenance of equipment to ensure that manufacturing specifications are met. Maintenance activities, including the date and individual(s) performing the maintenance activities, shall be documented.

(2) *Inspection.* Each manufacturer shall conduct periodic inspections in accordance with established procedures to ensure adherence to applicable equipment maintenance schedules. The inspections, including the date and individual(s) conducting the inspections, shall be documented.

(3) *Adjustment.* Each manufacturer shall ensure that any inherent limitations or allowable tolerances are visibly posted on or near equipment requiring periodic adjustments or are readily available to personnel performing these adjustments.

(h) *Manufacturing material.* Where a manufacturing material could reasonably be expected to have an adverse effect on product quality, the manufacturer shall establish and maintain procedures for the use and removal of such manufacturing material to ensure that it is removed or limited to an amount that does not adversely affect the device's quality. The removal or reduction of such manufacturing material shall be documented.

(i) *Automated processes.* When computers or automated data processing systems are used as part of production or the quality system, the manufacturer shall validate computer software for its intended use according to an established protocol. All software changes shall be validated before approval and issuance. These validation activities and results shall be documented.

§ 820.72 Inspection, measuring, and test equipment.

(a) *Control of inspection, measuring, and test equipment.* Each manufacturer shall ensure that all inspection, measuring, and test equipment, including mechanical, automated, or electronic inspection and test equipment, is suitable for its intended purposes and is capable of producing valid results. Each manufacturer shall establish and maintain procedures to ensure that equipment is routinely calibrated, inspected, checked, and maintained. The procedures shall include provisions for handling, preservation, and storage of equipment, so that its accuracy and fitness for use are maintained. These activities shall be documented.

(b) *Calibration.* Calibration procedures shall include specific directions and limits for accuracy and precision. When accuracy and precision limits are not met, there shall be provisions for remedial action to reestablish the limits and to evaluate whether there was any adverse effect on the device's quality. These activities shall be documented.

(1) *Calibration standards.* Calibration standards used for inspection, measuring, and test equipment shall be traceable to national or international standards. If national or international standards are not practical or available, the manufacturer shall use an independent reproducible standard. If no applicable standard exists, the manufacturer shall establish and maintain an in-house standard.

(2) *Calibration records.* The equipment identification, calibration dates, the individual performing each calibration, and the next calibration date shall be documented. These records shall be displayed on or near each piece of equipment or shall be readily available to the personnel using such equipment and to the individuals responsible for calibrating the equipment.

§ 820.75 Process validation.

(a) Where the results of a process cannot be fully verified by subsequent inspection and test, the process shall be validated with a high degree of assurance and approved according to established procedures. The validation activities and results, including the date and signature of the individual(s) approving the validation and where appropriate the major equipment validated, shall be documented.

(b) Each manufacturer shall establish and maintain procedures for monitoring and control of process parameters for validated processes to ensure that the specified requirements continue to be met.

(1) Each manufacturer shall ensure that validated processes are performed by qualified individual(s).

(2) For validated processes, the monitoring and control methods and data, the date performed, and, where appropriate, the individual(s) performing the process or the major equipment used shall be documented.

(c) When changes or process deviations occur, the manufacturer shall review and evaluate the process and perform revalidation where appropriate. These activities shall be documented.

SUBPART H - ACCEPTANCE ACTIVITIES

§ 820.80 Receiving, in-process, and finished device acceptance.

(a) *General.* Each manufacturer shall establish and maintain procedures for acceptance activities. Acceptance activities include inspections, tests, or other verification activities.

(b) *Receiving acceptance activities.* Each manufacturer shall establish and maintain procedures for acceptance of incoming product. Incoming product shall be inspected, tested, or otherwise verified as conforming to specified requirements. Acceptance or rejection shall be documented.

(c) *In-process acceptance activities.* Each manufacturer shall establish and maintain acceptance procedures, where appropriate, to ensure that specified requirements for in-process product are met. Such procedures shall ensure that in-process product is controlled until the required inspection and tests or other verification activities have been completed, or necessary approvals are received, and are documented.

(d) *Final acceptance activities.* Each manufacturer shall establish and maintain procedures for finished device acceptance to ensure that each production run, lot, or batch of finished devices meets acceptance criteria. Finished devices shall be held in quarantine or otherwise adequately controlled until released. Finished devices shall not be released for distribution until:

(1) The activities required in the DMR are completed;

(2) the associated data and documentation is reviewed;

(3) the release is authorized by the signature of a designated individual(s); and

(4) the authorization is dated.

(e) *Acceptance records.* Each manufacturer shall document acceptance activities required by this part. These records shall include:

(1) The acceptance activities performed;

(2) the dates acceptance activities are performed;

(3) the results;

(4) the signature of the individual(s) conducting the acceptance activities; and

(5) where appropriate the equipment used. These records shall be part of the DHR.

§ 820.86 Acceptance status.

Each manufacturer shall identify by suitable means the acceptance status of product, to indicate the conformance or nonconformance of product with acceptance criteria. The identification of acceptance status shall be maintained throughout manufacturing, packaging, labeling, installation, and servicing of the product to ensure that only product which has passed the required acceptance activities is distributed, used, or installed.

SUBPART I - NONCONFORMING PRODUCT

§ 820.90 Nonconforming product.

(a) *Control of nonconforming product.* Each manufacturer shall establish and maintain procedures to control product that does not conform to specified requirements. The procedures shall address the identification, documentation, evaluation, segregation, and disposition of nonconforming product. The evaluation of nonconformance shall include a determination of the need for an investigation and notification of the persons or organizations responsible for the nonconformance. The evaluation and any investigation shall be documented.

(b) *Nonconformity review and disposition.*

(1) Each manufacturer shall establish and maintain procedures that define the responsibility for review and the authority for the disposition of nonconforming product.

The procedures shall set forth the review and disposition process. Disposition of nonconforming product shall be documented. Documentation shall include the justification for use of nonconforming product and the signature of the individual(s) authorizing the use.

(2) Each manufacturer shall establish and maintain procedures for rework, to include retesting and reevaluation of the nonconforming product after rework, to ensure that the product meets its current approved specifications. Rework and reevaluation activities, including a determination of any adverse effect from the rework upon the product, shall be documented in the DHR.

SUBPART J - CORRECTIVE AND PREVENTIVE ACTION

§ 820.100 Corrective and preventive action.

(a) Each manufacturer shall establish and maintain procedures for implementing corrective and preventive action. The procedures shall include requirements for:

(1) Analyzing processes, work operations, concessions, quality audit reports, quality records, service records, complaints, returned product, and other sources of quality data to identify existing and potential causes of nonconforming product, or other quality problems. Appropriate statistical methodology shall be employed where necessary to detect recurring quality problems;

(2) Investigating the cause of nonconformities relating to product, processes, and the quality system;

(3) Identifying the action(s) needed to correct and prevent recurrence of nonconforming product and other quality problems;

(4) Verifying or validating the corrective and preventive action to ensure that such action is effective and does not adversely affect the finished device;

(5) Implementing and recording changes in methods and procedures needed to correct and prevent identified quality problems;

(6) Ensuring that information related to quality problems or nonconforming product is disseminated to those directly responsible for assuring the quality of such product or the prevention of such problems; and

(7) Submitting relevant information on identified quality problems, as well as corrective and preventive actions, for management review.

(b) All activities required under this section, and their results, shall be documented.

SUBPART K - LABELING AND PACKAGING CONTROL

§ 820.120 Device labeling.

Each manufacturer shall establish and maintain procedures to control labeling activities.

(a) *Label integrity.* Labels shall be printed and applied so as to remain legible and affixed during the customary conditions of processing, storage, handling, distribution, and where appropriate use.

(b) *Labeling inspection.* Labeling shall not be released for storage or use until a designated individual(s) has examined the labeling for accuracy including, where applicable, the correct unique device identifier (UDI) or universal product code (UPC), expiration date, control number, storage instructions, handling instructions, and any additional processing instructions. The release, including the date and signature of the individual(s) performing the examination, shall be documented in the DHR.

(c) *Labeling storage.* Each manufacturer shall store labeling in a manner that provides proper identification and is designed to prevent mixups.

(d) *Labeling operations.* Each manufacturer shall control labeling and packaging operations to prevent labeling mixups. The label and labeling used for each production unit, lot, or batch shall be documented in the DHR.

(e) *Control number.* Where a control number is required by § 820.65, that control number shall be on or shall accompany the device through distribution.

[61 FR 52654, Oct. 7, 1996, as amended at 78 FR 58822, Sept. 24, 2013]

§ 820.130 Device packaging.

Each manufacturer shall ensure that device packaging and shipping containers are designed and constructed to protect the device from alteration or damage during the customary conditions of processing, storage, handling, and distribution.

Subpart L - Handling, Storage, Distribution, and Installation

§ 820.140 Handling.

Each manufacturer shall establish and maintain procedures to ensure that mixups, damage, deterioration, contamination, or other adverse effects to product do not occur during handling.

§ 820.150 Storage.

(a) Each manufacturer shall establish and maintain procedures for the control of storage areas and stock rooms for product to prevent mixups, damage, deterioration, contamination, or other adverse effects pending use or distribution and to ensure that no obsolete, rejected, or deteriorated product is used or distributed. When the quality of product deteriorates over time, it shall be stored in a manner to facilitate proper stock rotation, and its condition shall be assessed as appropriate.

(b) Each manufacturer shall establish and maintain procedures that describe the methods for authorizing receipt from and dispatch to storage areas and stock rooms.

§ 820.160 Distribution.

(a) Each manufacturer shall establish and maintain procedures for control and distribution of finished devices to ensure that only those devices approved for release are distributed and that purchase orders are reviewed to ensure that ambiguities and errors are resolved before devices are released for distribution. Where a device's fitness for use or quality deteriorates over time, the procedures shall ensure that expired devices or devices deteriorated beyond acceptable fitness for use are not distributed.

(b) Each manufacturer shall maintain distribution records which include or refer to the location of:

(1) The name and address of the initial consignee;

(2) The identification and quantity of devices shipped;

(3) The date shipped; and

(4) Any control number(s) used.

§ 820.170 Installation.

(a) Each manufacturer of a device requiring installation shall establish and maintain adequate installation and inspection instructions, and where appropriate test procedures. Instructions and procedures shall include directions for ensuring proper installation so that the device will perform as intended after installation. The manufacturer shall distribute the instructions and procedures with the device or otherwise make them available to the person(s) installing the device.

(b) The person installing the device shall ensure that the installation, inspection, and any required testing are performed in accordance with the manufacturer's instructions and procedures and shall document the inspection and any test results to demonstrate proper installation.

SUBPART M - RECORDS

§ 820.180 General requirements.

All records required by this part shall be maintained at the manufacturing establishment or other location that is reasonably accessible to responsible officials of the manufacturer and to employees of FDA designated to perform inspections. Such records, including those not stored at the inspected establishment, shall be made readily available for review and copying by FDA employee(s). Such records shall be legible and shall be stored to minimize deterioration and to prevent loss. Those records stored in automated data processing systems shall be backed up.

(a) *Confidentiality.* Records deemed confidential by the manufacturer may be marked to aid FDA in determining whether information may be disclosed under the public information regulation in part 20 of this chapter.

(b) *Record retention period.* All records required by this part shall be retained for a period of time equivalent to the design and expected life of the device, but in no case less than 2 years from the date of release for commercial distribution by the manufacturer.

(c) *Exceptions.* This section does not apply to the reports required by § 820.20(c) Management review, § 820.22

Quality audits, and supplier audit reports used to meet the requirements of § 820.50(a) Evaluation of suppliers, contractors, and consultants, but does apply to procedures established under these provisions. Upon request of a designated employee of FDA, an employee in management with executive responsibility shall certify in writing that the management reviews and quality audits required under this part, and supplier audits where applicable, have been performed and documented, the dates on which they were performed, and that any required corrective action has been undertaken.

§ 820.181 Device master record.

Each manufacturer shall maintain device master records (DMR's). Each manufacturer shall ensure that each DMR is prepared and approved in accordance with § 820.40. The DMR for each type of device shall include, or refer to the location of, the following information:

(a) Device specifications including appropriate drawings, composition, formulation, component specifications, and software specifications;

(b) Production process specifications including the appropriate equipment specifications, production methods, production procedures, and production environment specifications;

(c) Quality assurance procedures and specifications including acceptance criteria and the quality assurance equipment to be used;

(d) Packaging and labeling specifications, including methods and processes used; and

(e) Installation, maintenance, and servicing procedures and methods.

§ 820.184 Device history record.

Each manufacturer shall maintain device history records (DHR's). Each manufacturer shall establish and maintain procedures to ensure that DHR's for each batch, lot, or unit are maintained to demonstrate that the device is manufactured in accordance with the DMR and the requirements of this part. The DHR shall include, or refer to the location of, the following information:

(a) The dates of manufacture;

(b) The quantity manufactured;

(c) The quantity released for distribution;

(d) The acceptance records which demonstrate the device is manufactured in accordance with the DMR;

(e) The primary identification label and labeling used for each production unit; and

(f) Any unique device identifier (UDI) or universal product code (UPC), and any other device identification(s) and control number(s) used.

[61 FR 52654, Oct. 7, 1996, as amended at 78 FR 58822, Sept. 24, 2013]

§ 820.186 Quality system record.

Each manufacturer shall maintain a quality system record (QSR). The QSR shall include, or refer to the location of, procedures and the documentation of activities required by this part that are not specific to a particular type of device(s), including, but not limited to, the records required by § 820.20. Each manufacturer shall ensure that the QSR is prepared and approved in accordance with § 820.40.

§ 820.198 Complaint files.

(a) Each manufacturer shall maintain complaint files. Each manufacturer shall establish and maintain procedures for receiving, reviewing, and evaluating complaints by a formally designated unit. Such procedures shall ensure that:

(1) All complaints are processed in a uniform and timely manner;

(2) Oral complaints are documented upon receipt; and

(3) Complaints are evaluated to determine whether the complaint represents an event which is required to be reported to FDA under part 803 of this chapter, Medical Device Reporting.

(b) Each manufacturer shall review and evaluate all complaints to determine whether an investigation is necessary. When no investigation is made, the manufacturer shall maintain a record that includes the reason no investigation was made and the name of the individual responsible for the decision not to investigate.

(c) Any complaint involving the possible failure of a device, labeling, or packaging to meet any of its specifications shall be reviewed, evaluated, and investigated, unless such investigation has already been performed for a similar complaint and another investigation is not necessary.

(d) Any complaint that represents an event which must be reported to FDA under part 803 of this chapter shall be promptly reviewed, evaluated, and investigated by a designated individual(s) and shall be maintained in a separate portion of the complaint files or otherwise clearly identified. In addition to the information required by § 820.198(e), records of investigation under this paragraph shall include a determination of:

(1) Whether the device failed to meet specifications;

(2) Whether the device was being used for treatment or diagnosis; and

(3) The relationship, if any, of the device to the reported incident or adverse event.

(e) When an investigation is made under this section, a record of the investigation shall be maintained by the formally designated unit identified in paragraph (a) of this section. The record of investigation shall include:

(1) The name of the device;

(2) The date the complaint was received;

(3) Any unique device identifier (UDI) or universal product code (UPC), and any other device identification(s) and control number(s) used;

(4) The name, address, and phone number of the complainant;

(5) The nature and details of the complaint;

(6) The dates and results of the investigation;

(7) Any corrective action taken; and

(8) Any reply to the complainant.

(f) When the manufacturer's formally designated complaint unit is located at a site separate from the manufacturing establishment, the investigated complaint(s) and the record(s) of investigation shall be reasonably accessible to the manufacturing establishment.

(g) If a manufacturer's formally designated complaint unit is located outside of the United States, records required by this section shall be reasonably accessible in the United States at either:

(1) A location in the United States where the manufacturer's records are regularly kept; or

(2) The location of the initial distributor.

[61 FR 52654, Oct. 7, 1996, as amended at 69 FR 11313, Mar. 10, 2004; 71 FR 16228, Mar. 31, 2006; 78 FR 58822, Sept. 24, 2013]

Subpart N - Servicing

§ 820.200 Servicing.

(a) Where servicing is a specified requirement, each manufacturer shall establish and maintain instructions and procedures for performing and verifying that the servicing meets the specified requirements.

(b) Each manufacturer shall analyze service reports with appropriate statistical methodology in accordance with § 820.100.

(c) Each manufacturer who receives a service report that represents an event which must be reported to FDA under part 803 of this chapter shall automatically consider the report a complaint and shall process it in accordance with the requirements of § 820.198.

(d) Service reports shall be documented and shall include:

(1) The name of the device serviced;

(2) Any unique device identifier (UDI) or universal product code (UPC), and any other device identification(s) and control number(s) used;

(3) The date of service;

(4) The individual(s) servicing the device;

(5) The service performed; and

(6) The test and inspection data.

[61 FR 52654, Oct. 7, 1996, as amended at 69 FR 11313, Mar. 10, 2004; 78 FR 58822, Sept. 24, 2013]

SUBPART O - STATISTICAL TECHNIQUES

§ 820.250 Statistical techniques.

(a) Where appropriate, each manufacturer shall establish and maintain procedures for identifying valid statistical techniques required for establishing, controlling, and verifying the acceptability of process capability and product characteristics.

(b) Sampling plans, when used, shall be written and based on a valid statistical rationale. Each manufacturer shall establish and maintain procedures to ensure that sampling methods are adequate for their intended use and to ensure that when changes occur the sampling plans are reviewed. These activities shall be documented.

Made in the USA
Columbia, SC
05 October 2024